WHAT GIANTS THEY WERE

New York Giants Greats Talk About Their Teams, Their Coaches, and the Times of Their Lives

RICHARD WHITTINGHAM

INTRODUCTION BY WELLINGTON MARA

TRIUMPH
BOOKS
CHICAGO

This book is available in quantity at special discounts for your group or organization. For further information, contact:

Triumph Books
601 South LaSalle Street
Suite 500
Chicago, Illinois 60605
(312) 939-3330
Fax (312) 663-3557

Printed in the United States

ISBN 1-57243-368-X

Book design by Eileen Wagner

Table of Contents

Acknowledgments

There are certain perks that go along with the creation of a book like this that are immeasurable and irreplaceable:

Like sitting around a table one induction weekend at the Pro Football Hall of Fame with Mel Hein, Johnny Blood McNally, and Don Hutson, listening to their stories of what the game used to be like when helmets were soft and no one left the playing field when the ball changed hands.

Or, wandering with Shipwreck Kelly through his Gatsby-like mansion on Long Island Sound as he speaks of coming to New York from the pastures of Kentucky, playing football, and, in the hours he wasn't on the field, cabareting in the city's most famous watering holes along with pals like Jock Whitney, Dan Topping, and Bing Crosby.

And, of course, being in Wellington Mara's office as he pulls Giants stories from his encyclopedic mind, spanning from that first morning in 1925 when he was nine years old and heard his father say, "I'm going to try to put pro football over in New York today," all the way to the Super Bowls at the other end of the team's glorious history.

A book of this nature would not be possible without the generous help of many people. The author would especially like to thank Wellington Mara and the New York Giants organization. Thanks also to the Pro Football Hall of Fame in Canton, Ohio, notably Joe Horrigan, curator and archivist. And of course, all those former Giants, legends in their own right, who shared their stories with the author: Red Badgro, Rosey Brown, Charlie Conerly, Benny Friedman, Frank Gifford, Mel Hein, Sam Huff, Jim Katcavage, Shipwreck Kelly, Tom Landry, Tuffy Leemans, Dick Lynch, Dick Modzelewski, Harry Newman, Andy Robustelli, Kyle Rote, Phil Simms, Pat Summerall, Y. A. Tittle, Alex Webster, and Arnie Weinmeister.

Introduction

WELLINGTON MARA

My earliest recollection of the Giants was on a Sunday morning in the autumn of 1925; I was about nine years old. We were coming out of mass, and I remember my father saying to one of his friends, "I'm gonna try to put pro football over in New York today." Then I recall going to the game. I don't think my father had ever seen a football game before.

During the game—and I've told the story many times—we were sitting on the Giants' side of the field, and it was a little chilly. My mother complained to my father that we were sitting in the shade. Why couldn't we go over and sit in the sun where we'd be nice and warm? So, the next game, and from then on, the Giants' sideline in the Polo Grounds was in the sun.

Another thing I remember from those first days was that I wanted to sit on the bench, and I got to. I remember our coach, Bob Folwell, a former Navy coach, turning to one of the players on the bench—his name was Paul Jappe—and saying, "Jappe, get in there and give 'em hell!" I thought, boy, this is really a rough game.

My father came to own the Giants in a kind of roundabout way. He was a bookmaker in New York, and he was very friendly with Billy Gibson, who was the manager of Gene Tunney, the boxer. My father had actually been instrumental in Tunney's early career. He also had been very friendly from boyhood with Al Smith, and through him with the political organization in New York City and New York state, and boxing at that time was very politically oriented. My father helped Tunney to get some fights that he otherwise might not have been able to get.

Billy Gibson came into my father's office one day and brought with him a gentleman named Harry A. March, who was a retired army doctor. Dr. March had been interested in pro football and its origins out in Ohio—the Canton area. There had not been a pro football team in New York before that time, although I've heard that Jimmy Jemail, a columnist back then for the *New York Daily News*—he wrote "The Inquiring Reporter"—claimed that he had a team in New York in 1924 and that my father took over that franchise.

From what I heard later there was talk about buying an NFL franchise. I heard that my father simply said, "How much will it cost?" and that was it. There are two versions of the answer to that: one was that it was $500, the other that it was

Longtime head coach Steve Owen (1931–53) accepts a silver service on his retirement. The Mara family looks on; from left, Wellington, Tim, and Jack.

$2,500. I know my father did say something to the effect that an empty store in New York City was worth that, whichever figure it was, and that's how he got into pro football.

Pro football in New York was very unsuccessful at first. My father's friends all told him that he was foolish to stay with it. I remember Governor Al Smith in our house one day after the team had just lost rather badly to Green Bay. Al Smith said to my father, "Your team will never amount to anything. Why don't you give it up?" My father looked at Jack and me and said, "The boys would run me right out of the house if I did."

Money was very tight in the '30s. However, according to my father, compared to other areas of the entertainment business, sports somewhat prospered during the Depression because they really offered the best entertainment for the money. A football game or a baseball game was great entertainment, and a man could afford to bring his whole family. Still, the Giants were just barely breaking even in the mid-1930s.

Of course, football was a very different game back then. I recall the days when you didn't have hash marks at all, and a little later when you did but to get the ball placed on one of them you actually had to go out of bounds. If you were tackled one yard from the sideline, that was where the ball was put in play. I remember teams having special plays for that. Along those lines, I remember Tony Plansky, a tailback from Georgetown, who had been a great decathlon athlete, drop-kicking a field goal for us from around the 40-yard line that won a game. The thing was, however, that he was way over to the left side of the field. He was ambidextrous and kicked it with his left foot, where ordinarily he did his kicking right-footed.

It was also a one-platoon game then. As Steve Owen used to say, men were men in those days. He was our great coach for so many years, and he saw a lot of truly sturdy, talented, sixty-minute men who played for and against us. Stamina played a big role in those days, and the players had to pace themselves. They couldn't go all out on every play—you just couldn't do that for sixty minutes of football–playing time. The players against you were under the same handicap, but it still was grueling.

The war came along and took the great majority of the athletes out of the NFL. It threatened to close down pro football altogether. George Halas was going back into the navy, and since he was going to be gone from football he kind of led a drive to cancel the season, call the whole thing off. George Marshall, owner of the Redskins, Bert Bell, owner of the Steelers, and my father crusaded to keep it going at any cost, even if we had to play 4-Fs and high school players, which we in fact did. It may very well be that playing under those circumstances helped to save the NFL, because when the war was over Arch Ward started the All-America Football Conference. It started at a terrible disadvantage because we were already established. I think if we had suspended operations for three or four years and then tried to start it up again, the AAFC would have started on more equal terms with us, and the league might be a very different one from what it is today.

The game changed considerably after the war. The offenses became more sophisticated, there was a lot more passing, and the players were getting bigger and faster all the time.

We had some of our most noteworthy and memorable teams in the 1950s and early '60s. Jim Lee Howell, our head coach for much of that time, had the best pair of assistants ever under one roof: Vince Lombardi handling the offense and Tom Landry the defense. With Charlie Conerly and later Y. A. Tittle quarterbacking, backs like Frank Gifford and Alex Webster, and pass catchers of the caliber of Kyle Rote and

Del Shofner, we provided a lot of exciting offense. And the defense! It was simply one of the best of all time: Andy Robustelli, Sam Huff, Rosey Grier, Em Tunnell, Dick Modzelewski, Jim Katcavage, Dick Lynch, Jimmy Patton, and others.

Certainly the game was less rewarding financially in those early days. Most of the players and coaches had to get other jobs to survive. Vince Lombardi had an off-season job with a bank when he was with us in the late 1950s. The game was still great fun, though, and the men who played it were very memorable.

Nothing, however, has been more gratifying than watching the Giants of 1986 march through the season and the playoffs to the Super Bowl and triumph there in the Rose Bowl Stadium [39–20 over Denver], and the Giants of 1990 repeating this victory down in Tampa [20–19 over Buffalo], giving us two world championships in five years.

We've been around for quite some time now and many great players have come and gone. They've given us a wonderful store of memories. They really were Giants, in all senses of the word.

WHAT GIANTS
THEY WERE

1 College Days

One of the most gifted Giants ever, Frank Gifford, carries the ball here against the Cleveland Browns. Gifford, who starred as a halfback and a flanker during his twelve years with the Giants (1952-60, '62-64), was inducted into the Pro Football Hall of Fame in 1977. Other Giants in the picture are Kyle Rote (No. 44) and guard Darrell Dess (No. 62).

GIFFORD at USC

It had been a great experience at USC. My coach at Bakersfield High School, a man by the name of Homer Beattie, had played for USC and at that time he was certainly one of the most important persons in my life. He got me going in the right direction academically as well as on the football field. I hadn't been the greatest of students. He felt I could possibly play for USC, and he knew I would have to qualify on both levels if I were to be accepted at that school.

After my fourth year at Bakersfield, USC did indeed offer me a football scholarship, but I was deficient in a few academic units and I had to make them up. So I went for a year to Bakersfield Junior College and then moved on to USC.

At USC, they never really could find just what to do with me. I had played offense and defense in high school and ended up a T-formation quarterback my junior year. I played safety on defense. And in my senior year they switched to a wing T and I became a running back. Then in junior college we had an offense where I both ran and passed the ball.

So, at USC I didn't exactly fit anywhere in particular. For two years I played defense. Then in my senior year they brought in a new coach, Jess Hill, and he designed an offense that was pretty much suited to me, a single wing and a wing T, and I was sort of the focus of it, running and passing and receiving. He also had a fine staff with Mel Hein and Don Clark, who would later become head coach at Southern Cal. And it made a big difference. We were 3–7–0 in 1950, my junior year, and won our first seven games in 1951. The fifth game that we won that year was over the University of California, and at the time they were ranked number one in the nation and had a thirty-nine-game winning streak. Well, after that all the bells went off and we jumped from nothing to something like fourth or fifth in the nation. Suddenly the press and the media were all over the campus, and a week later I was being photographed for All-American. It was the weirdest thing—we all kept wondering how it happened so fast.

We didn't go to the Rose Bowl because we lost our last three games that year, but I did play in the East-West Game and the Senior Bowl. As I learned later, Wellington Mara had scouted both those games. Mel Hein had told him to take a close look at me. That's really how they scouted in those days. There weren't any combines or things like that, or even scouting departments for the individual teams. People like Wellington Mara relied on coaches they knew, former players, and they listened to their recommendations.

> "Suddenly the press and the media were all over the campus, and a week later I was being photographed for All-American. It was the weirdest thing—we all kept wondering how it happened so fast."
> —FRANK GIFFORD

LANDRY at Texas

It was in the summer of 1950 when I officially joined the Giants. I was twenty-five years old at the time, a little old for a rookie in the NFL, but there were several things that had come up before my entering the NFL.

I had attended the University of Texas after playing football in high school down in south Texas along the border there, in a town called Mission. There was an oilman in our town who was a Texas U. graduate, and he was the one who got me an interview with the university.

In those days, D. X. Bible [also known as Dana Xenophon Bible] was the coach there, and they had a tremendous program under him. That was around 1941 and 1942. They were anticipating a national championship in 1941, and *Life* magazine featured them in a big article as the nation's top team. After that they lost three games.

Tom Landry, a ball carrier in this publicity shot, played defensive back for the Giants from 1950 through 1955 and was acknowledged as one of the finest in the league. He was named All-Pro in 1954. Landry served as player-defensive coach in 1954 and 1955 and as full-time defensive coordinator from 1956 through 1959 before leaving to take over the head coaching duties at the newly enfranchised Dallas Cowboys in 1960.

I came there the next year, and D. X. Bible was still the coach. I played in 1942 but then I went into the Army Air Corps in February 1943. I came back and reentered school at the university in the spring of 1945. So my sophomore year was actually the 1946 season. That, as it turned out, was D. X. Bible's last year—he had actually been coaching in the college ranks since 1913.

When I came up into the varsity that year, we were playing D. X. Bible's single wing and I was pegged at fullback and defensive back. The next year Blair Cherry took over as head coach, and he moved me into a quarterback position behind Bobby Layne. So I played first-string defensive back and second-string quarterback. But I busted up the thumb on my right hand and the joint kind of froze up on me, so I couldn't play quarterback anymore. Coach Cherry moved me back to fullback then. But let's face it—nobody was going to beat out Bobby Layne at quarterback.

TITTLE at LSU

I was born and raised in Marshall, Texas, which is where I started playing football. It was in junior high—that was about 1938.

I ended up going to LSU. Marshall is right near the Louisiana border, and during the war my brother was going to Tulane in New Orleans—he was an outstanding blocking back. They were big rivals with LSU in those days. I went over to see him play at LSU in Baton Rouge and I was impressed with the campus there.

But the main reason I chose LSU was because they let freshmen play on the varsity team in those days. The other colleges didn't. I felt I could play a lot the first year and, in fact, I did. I had offers from the University of Texas, Rice, Tulsa, TCU—but in those schools I couldn't play right off.

The talented toe of Pat Summerall. From 1958 through 1961, he handled all the placekicking chores for the Giants, contributing a total of 223 points to the team on fifty-nine field goals and forty-six extra points. During his ten-year NFL career, Summerall also played defensive end and occasionally offensive end.

SUMMERALL at Arkansas

I went on a lot of college recruiting trips as a high school senior. In those days you could go and put on a uniform and work out with the college teams, a lot of things like that. The NCAA rules have changed considerably since then. The two places that I was invited to and was most serious about were West Point and the University of Florida. West Point, I thought when I went there, looked a little too much like a jail. They were also suggesting that they would be sending me first to Kentucky Military Institute to study to be sure I could pass Army's entrance exams—my high school grades weren't all that good. Adding these things up, I decided I didn't really want to go there.

At the University of Florida, they wanted me to play both basketball and football. At that time it was relatively easy to do that because the seasons were shorter and the quality of both games was not nearly what it is today. Anyway, I didn't want to do that.

At the same time, my high school football coach, a gentleman named Hobart Hooser, had been hired by the University of Arkansas as their line coach. Well, he had been kind of like a father to me. He came back down to Florida and talked to me about going to Arkansas, and I went.

It was at Arkansas where I really got started as a kicker. When I was a sophomore—that must have been 1949—the coaching staff was not happy with the guy who was kicking off, no field goals or extra points. They said anyone who'd like to try kicking should come on out thirty minutes early this one day. Well, I said, what the heck—I'll give it a try. So I did. And it seemed to be something that was very natural to me. From then on, I kicked off for Arkansas.

At the same time I was playing offensive and defensive end, the kind of thing you did in those days. The squads were just so much smaller. When I was with the Chicago Cardinals we were limited to thirty-three players on the roster, and with the Giants it was thirty-five. A team could not afford to have a specialist on its roster who did nothing other than kick or punt.

I had no thoughts of being a specialist back then. If you aspired to play professional football, the ultimate was to play the game, offense and defense. Kicking was just an additional element.

One of the highlights at Arkansas, I remember, was beating Texas my senior year [1951], and I got to kick the game-winning field goal that day. Beating Texas was the biggest thrill you could have down there in those days. Actually, field goals around that time were relatively unheard of. I kicked the most in college that year—just barely beat out Vic Janowicz of Ohio State, who won the Heisman Trophy—I kicked four.

HEIN at Washington State

I had an older brother over at Washington State who was on the football team, and he told the coach, Babe Hollingberry, about me and that I was a pretty good football player. Well, they looked up my records, and the coach made some long-distance calls to us in Bellingham. I told him I didn't want to go to Washington State. But finally he talked my father into it, and my father talked me into going there.

We had a championship freshman team, and most of the freshmen went on the next year to start on the varsity. We had a good season as juniors—only lost two games. And as seniors we went to the Rose Bowl. That was the last time Washington State played in a Rose Bowl game—1931—and we played Alabama. In those days, they selected teams from different parts of the country, not just the Pac Ten and Big Ten like they do today.

One of pro football's all-time greats, center Mel Hein was the twenty-third charter member of the Pro Football Hall of Fame. He was named All-Pro eight consecutive years (1933–40), and only Phil Simms (1979–93) has ever played in as many seasons as the fifteen memorable ones that Hein turned in (1931–45).

There's one thing I'll always remember from that game. Our coach, Babe Hollingberry, was somewhat of a showman, and he was superstitious. In the showman role he brought a lot of new bright crimson red uniforms for our appearance in the Rose Bowl—the headgear was red, the shoes were red, the stockings were red, everything was red. I think it scared us more than Alabama because we didn't play too good a ball game—they walloped us 24–0. They simply had a better team than we had.

The superstitious part of Babe Hollingberry came out when we got back to Pullman, the city where Washington State's campus is located, after the game. No one ever saw those uniforms again, and the story is that Babe had a big bonfire and burned them all. He didn't want any of his teams ever to wear those uniforms again.

ROBUSTELLI at Arnold College

After the service I went to a little college in Milford, Connecticut, named Arnold, which no longer exists. I got out of the service about six or seven months after the war ended, early 1946. Most colleges around were crowded with veterans who had already returned from the war. I think I could have gotten into Fordham, but they wanted me to go to a prep school to pick up a couple of credits. I'd gone from high school before graduating to LaSalle Military Academy for three months before going into the service. I had to wait until I was eighteen before enlisting, so by doing that I missed a few high school credits, and that's what Fordham wanted me to make up.

A couple of my buddies were going up to Arnold College because they were having difficulty getting into the better-known colleges too. I went along with them. I was on the GI Bill of Rights, and so at Arnold they said come on in. It was primarily a phys ed school, but before there were about two hundred girls and only about forty boys. With the veterans now coming in, it ended up with more boys and less girls—about 350 students in all.

I decided to enroll, and once there it gave me the opportunity to play any sport I wanted to. So I played football and baseball. We played football against schools like the Coast Guard Academy, St. Michael's in Vermont, Adelphi on Long Island, and a lot of teachers' colleges. It wasn't the greatest competition in the world, but still it was tough football.

HUFF at West Virginia

The University of West Virginia recruited me when I was a senior. Art Lewis was the head coach there then, and he came and talked to me about coming to West Virginia. He came to our house and to the high school; he was very professional about recruiting. However, the first to talk to me was an assistant coach, Harold "Toad" Lahr, who left shortly thereafter to take the head coaching job at Colgate.

Both the University of Florida and Army were also interested, and I visited both campuses. Florida, in Gainesville, was really nice. You had to like it there with the weather, the palm trees—especially coming from West Virginia. But I really wanted to go to West Virginia, which is in Morgantown—that was always my dream. I played both ways in college—offensive and defensive tackle. I didn't switch to linebacker until I got with the Giants. They thought I was too small to play tackle in the pros, and rightly so.

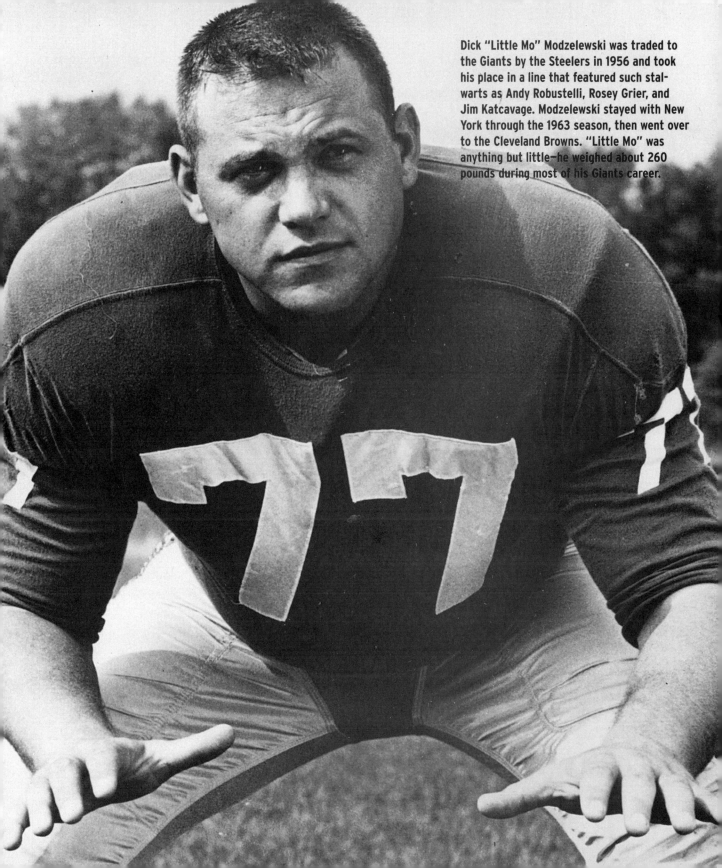

Dick "Little Mo" Modzelewski was traded to the Giants by the Steelers in 1956 and took his place in a line that featured such stalwarts as Andy Robustelli, Rosey Grier, and Jim Katcavage. Modzelewski stayed with New York through the 1963 season, then went over to the Cleveland Browns. "Little Mo" was anything but little—he weighed about 260 pounds during most of his Giants career.

MODZELEWSKI at Maryland

"Coach Tatum always said my father was Maryland's good-luck charm."

—DICK MODZELEWSKI

My brother Ed and I went to Maryland. I had a number of offers because I'd been all-state my senior year. Notre Dame was interested in me; so were Tennessee, Pittsburgh, and South Carolina. I'll never forget South Carolina. My dad was home one day—my dad was an immigrant, and all he could write was his name—and a coach from South Carolina pulled up in front of our house in a brand-new 1949 green Oldsmobile convertible. And I was told if I went to school down there, there was a good chance I'd get me a car like that. Well, my old man about flipped. He said he couldn't believe it, him working in the coal mines all those years and here is his son, a senior in high school and they're offering him a car like that. It was hard to turn down, but I did.

Coach Jim Tatum came over from Maryland and talked to my parents, and I think he did a good job selling them. Part of it, of course, was how good it would be with Ed already there. So that's where I went, and I'm glad I did. I had the benefit of a great coach [Tatum] there.

Coach Tatum always said my father was Maryland's good-luck charm. When Ed and I were playing there, a friend of mine, Dom Corso, used to bring my father to all the home games. He would wait for my dad to come from the coal mine on Friday, drive him to College Park, and then after mass on Sunday drive him back. After a while, Coach Tatum had my dad sit on the bench each time he came. Tatum loved my dad.

My dad said his proudest moment was when my brother Ed and I were invited to a big sports lunch at the White House. This was at the end of my senior year, 1953, and my brother was in the air force at the time. Ed got his invitation out at Hamilton Air Force Base in California and told his commanding officer he had to go to Washington for this lunch at the White House with Dwight D. Eisenhower. His CO just laughed at him, but when he showed him the invitation they got a jet ready and flew his butt to Washington for the lunch. It was a big affair, with people like Rocky Marciano and Joe DiMaggio and Florence Chadwick there. It was a big thrill for Ed and me, and I think maybe even bigger for my dad getting to tell everyone around town where his two boys were having lunch.

CONERLY at Ole Miss

"... all told, it was a real good year."

—CHARLIE CONERLY

I was born and raised in Clarksdale, Mississippi. Went to Clarksdale Bobo High School there—I don't know what the Bobo stands for; somebody, I guess, just named it that.

In 1941 I went to Ole Miss—the University of Mississippi. Then in 1943 I went into the Marines. I was overseas for a little more than two years and got out early in 1946.

I was supposed to have graduated from college in 1945, and that year the Washington Redskins drafted me. Only problem was that I was over in Guam. They sent me a telegram down in Mississippi, which my mother got. She wrote me about it, and I said to myself, "Well, I'd be happy to come back right away." But, of course, I couldn't.

After I got out of the Marines, I went back to Ole Miss and finished up there after the 1947 season. I played football in the fall of 1946 and then

Charlie Conerly (1948–61) quarterbacked the Giants throughout the 1950s. Throwing to receivers such as Kyle Rote, Frank Gifford, Alex Webster, and Bob Schnelker, he set every career passing record in Giants' history, all of which stood until Phil Simms came along in the 1980s.

again in 1947. My senior year [1947] we won the Southeastern Conference. I happily remember we beat Tennessee that year. Ole Miss had never beaten them before. [General Bob] Neyland was their coach. We played them up in Memphis and beat them pretty good [43–13]. Because we won the conference we should have gone to the Sugar Bowl, but earlier that year they announced a new bowl, the Delta Bowl, and Ole Miss accepted an invitation to it midway through our season. So we couldn't go to New Orleans—Alabama went instead to play Texas. We beat Texas Christian at the Delta Bowl [13–9], although we would've preferred beating Texas at the Sugar Bowl. But, all told, it was a real good year.

Kyle Rote carries the ball for the Giants in this 1953 game at the Polo Grounds. Rote (1951–61) started out as halfback with the Giants, but banged-up knees forced him to switch to flanker in 1952, where he became one of the Giants' best pass receivers. No. 31 is New York fullback Eddie Price.

ROTE at SMU

It was in San Antonio, Texas, where I grew up, that I started playing football. I attended Thomas Jefferson High School and played football and basketball; we went to the state championships in both my senior year.

Then I went to Vanderbilt University in Tennessee, where I thought I might play football. They had a summer program there, which enabled freshmen to become eligible for the varsity. And I thought that was a pretty good idea. We had to be enrolled before September, however. Well, I got up there in Nashville and my first thoughts were that I didn't see myself living in that part of the country after college.

Red Sanders was the head coach at Vanderbilt then, and he was a great recruiter. He'd been there since like 1940, and this was 1947. Later, of course, he would go on to make quite a name for himself coaching at UCLA. I went in one night to talk to him and explained that I was going to head back to San Antonio and that I had appreciated what he'd done for me, but I thought Texas was really the place for me.

It wasn't your classic case of being homesick; I was just concerned about the four years I would be spending up there and then going back to my friends and former teammates in Texas. He asked me to give it some thought, which I did. And then I booked myself on a train back to Texas. Ironically enough, as I was going back by train to Texas, four of my closest teammates were driving up to Vanderbilt. They had been invited by Coach Sanders. Anyway, they arrived and were looking all over for me, but I was headed back to Texas. When I got to San Antonio, they were in Nashville.

But it was a good decision on my part. I had a kind of standing offer at Southern Methodist—for basketball as well as football. So I went up to Dallas and talked to the football coach, Matty Bell; I asked him if the offer was still on the table, and he said the scholarship was still open. Between that and the fact that my girlfriend, who was to become my wife, was also planning to go there, the decision was not a very difficult one.

Doak Walker was already there at SMU—he was a year ahead of me—and he had already been in the military service too. Doak was a fabulous ballplayer. He won the Heisman Trophy when he was a junior [1948]. Doak had made All-American three years in a row—as a sophomore, junior, and senior. He was a tough act to follow.

We had been playing our games at a little stadium on the SMU campus back then, but with all the publicity Doak was getting it wasn't big enough. So they moved our home games into the Cotton Bowl down there in Dallas. We went from a campus-type sport to the major leagues, so to speak. Like they called Yankee Stadium "The House That Ruth Built," they got to calling the Cotton Bowl "The House That Walker Built."

After freshman ball, I played two years with Doak [1948 and 1949]. We went to the Cotton Bowl after the 1948 season and beat Oregon [21–13], whose quarterback that year was Norm Van Brocklin. Both Doak and I scored a touchdown in that game.

There was also a very memorable game the next year when we played Notre Dame at the Cotton Bowl, the last game of the 1949 regular season. They were

• 15 •

ranked number one in the nation at the time—in fact, Notre Dame hadn't lost a game since the last one of the 1945 season—and they had a bunch of All-Americans on the team: Bob Williams at quarterback, Emil Sitko at halfback, and Leon Hart and Jim Martin were their ends.

We had lost three games in the Southwest Conference, and on top of that Doak was injured and wouldn't be able to play at all. We were a definite underdog [the spread was twenty-eight points]. When the team arrived in Dallas, their coach, Frank Leahy, said, "We come here to round off a perfect season."

There was really a lot of money floating around Texas at that time—the oil business was booming. And the SMU backers had a lot of it. The game was played on December 3, a week after most all the other college teams had ended their seasons. And it was on national television and on armed-forces radio overseas. The SMU supporters took one look at that twenty-eight-point spread, and a lot of money went down on us. Word was they were betting the farm on SMU, or maybe the oil patch.

I filled in for Doak at tailback, and it turned into a great game. We shook their confidence. We were losing 13–0 at the half, but we came back very strong. In the fourth quarter we tied it up at twenty apiece. They got another touchdown to take the lead. I got hurt and had to come out but came back in a little later and got us down to their 4-yard line. They were thinking I was going to run the ball and keyed for it, but I was really beat up by that time. I tried a little jump pass and Jerry Groom intercepted it, and that was the game [27–20, Notre Dame]; but we gave them a heckuva scare. [Rote scored all three of the Mustangs' touchdowns that day.] *The Dallas Morning News* the next day had a headline: SMU WINS 20–27. And even if we didn't win, all those guys in Dallas who bet on us made a killing.

In 1950 Doak went on to the Detroit Lions and I took over full-time as tailback. We didn't have any games my senior year quite as exciting as the '49 Notre Dame game, but we had some good ones. We went up to Ohio State—they had Vic Janowicz at tailback, and he won the Heisman Trophy that year—and they were highly ranked. But we won up there in Columbus [32–27]. We won six of our ten games that year but didn't do too well in our conference.

BROWN at Morgan State

I was born in Charlottesville, Virginia, and that's where I went to school. I played football in high school—offensive and defensive tackle—and after my senior year the coach from Morgan State College in Baltimore came down and offered me a scholarship. My mother thought that was a fine thing, and she said that's where I would be going. In those days, the mothers made the decisions; nowadays it's more the kids who make the decisions.

So I went on up to Morgan State in 1949. I actually started college when I was fifteen, and I graduated when I was nineteen.

In those days, Morgan was an all-black school. And they had a very good football team then—I believe they had won something like fifty-two straight games by the time I arrived. We played against other all-black schools, like Virginia State College; Virginia Union; Hampton College, which was also in Virginia; Howard University, in Washington, D.C., and schools like that—mostly from that area.

One game I particularly remember from that time was against Central State College, which was in Wilberforce, Ohio. We both traveled to New York to play each other at the Polo Grounds. We were the first two black schools to play outside of our conference. That was my very first trip to New York.

Rosey Brown (No. 79) gets a breather. One of the game's all-time great offensive linemen, Brown played tackle for the Giants for thirteen years (1953–65). He earned All-Pro honors eight times and was invited to ten Pro Bowls. Brown was enshrined in the Pro Football Hall of Fame in 1975.

Coming from Virginia to Baltimore was something, but nothing like coming to New York for the first time. The only way I can explain it is like I was starry-eyed, taking in something I'd never seen the likes of before.

"... it was a
place where I
felt I would
really have a
chance to
play."

—ALEX WEBSTER

WEBSTER at North Carolina State

My first encounter with organized football was back in Kearny, New Jersey—
which is just north of Newark—where I was born and raised. That's where I
started playing the game in junior high school and then, of course, high school.

I was lucky to have gotten a whole bunch of scholarship offers after finishing
school in Kearny. I took a couple of trips to see the colleges. I went over to
Tennessee in Knoxville and down to University of Miami and a couple of other
schools. Then I went to take a look at North Carolina State, which is in Raleigh—
there's that whole complex of universities in the area there with North Carolina
in Chapel Hill and Duke in Durham, all neighbors.

Well, I really liked that area of the country, and the university was very appeal-
ing. The coach there was Beattie Feathers, who had gone to Tennessee and later was
a fine running back for the Chicago Bears. In fact, he was the first running back
in the NFL to gain more than one thousand yards rushing in a single season
[1,004 in the thirteen-game season of 1934]. Of course, he had Bronko Nagurski
blocking for him that year, which helped considerably.

There was a fellow by the name of Al Rotella, who was originally from New
Jersey but had gone to Tennessee and was now an assistant coach under Beattie at
North Carolina State. In fact, all of Beattie's staff were former Tennessee ballplayers. It was Al Rotella who recruited me, got me to go down to the school, and
introduced me to Beattie Feathers.

Well, Beattie had a wonderful heart, and he made me feel I had a good deal
of potential in his system at North Carolina State. So I took their offer, and it was
a good decision. My father had died when I was nine years old, and Beattie
became just like a father to me. He and the whole coaching staff there were great.

North Carolina State was not a big school in those days, back in the early 1950s.
It was basically an engineering and agricultural school. And it was a place where I
felt I would really have a chance to play. They were still playing the single wing and
that's what I had played in high school back in New Jersey. I'd been the tailback, and
I also played free safety on defense. State was playing the old Tennessee system with
the balanced line that General [Bob] Neyland had developed. It focused on running
out of the single wing, and that was good for me because as a senior in high school
I had suffered a shoulder separation and I wasn't throwing the football very well.
Running was what I wanted to do and what I did best.

I had a good four years down there in North Carolina. I played tailback and
free safety, just like high school, and we did pretty well. That's where I got the

Alex Webster was the Giants' premier running back from 1955 through 1964. He ended up with most of the team's rushing records when he retired after the 1964 season. Webster came back to the Giants as head coach from 1969 through 1973.

Y. A. Tittle hands off to fullback Alex Webster.

nickname "Big Red." I had red hair back then and my face was always red because of the simple fact that I was fair-skinned and was out in the sun so much down there. I think my head looked like a big red apple most of the time. Anyway, that old nickname has stuck through all the years.

KELLY at Kentucky

I went to the University of Kentucky, and I thought I was hot shit—but they didn't. I knew I could play football and that I could run like hell. But the coaches there hardly ever let me play.

Finally they put me in during the last freshman game of the season against Centre, which was a smaller school in Kentucky. I made three touchdowns after they let me in the game that day, and from that time on they knew I could play.

It was while I was at Kentucky that I got the nickname "Shipwreck." Around that time there was a man who was known as Shipwreck Kelly, an old sailor who went around sitting on flagpoles. He came to Lexington one day and climbed up and stood on a flagpole, and people thought that was very funny. I guess I was a

> "I knew I could play football and that I could run like hell."
>
> —SHIPWRECK KELLY

• 20 •

junior or senior then and a pretty big hotshot. Well, after we won a game, somebody said something like, "You can sure play football, but you can't sit on a flagpole like Shipwreck Kelly."

I said, "Bullshit." And I climbed up on a flagpole and stood there on top for a few minutes. Then I started down and somebody yelled, "What are you coming down for?"

"I have to piss," I said.

By the time I got to New York, after I graduated, I was known mostly as Shipwreck because I had climbed that flagpole.

BADGRO at USC

Howard Jones was the [football] coach of the USC Trojans [when I was there], and they had a wonderful football program. At the time, they and Notre Dame were two of the greatest teams in the country. This was in the mid-1920s. We played some very good football out there on the coast. Besides us, California had a good team. So did Stanford. They had Ernie Nevers then, and he was one of the all-time greats, and the famous Pop Warner was their coach.

I have a particular memory of [Nevers] out

Morris "Red" Badgro played end for the Giants from 1928 through 1935 and was named to three of the first four NFL All-Pro teams. In the words of another redhead, the immortal Red Grange, "Red was one of the best half-dozen ends I ever saw." He was inducted into the Pro Football Hall of Fame in 1981.

there. One year we would have gone to the Rose Bowl if it weren't for him. Nevers was punting out of his own end zone. We were losing, 13–12, late in the game, and a safety would win it for us. Well, we put on quite a rush, and Jeff Cravath, our center, blocked Ernie's kick. I was right alongside him, and, crazily, the ball bounced back up into Nevers's hands. If either Jeff or I had come up with the ball we would have gone to the Rose Bowl. But Ernie had it and ran the ball out for a first down.

Another wonderful player out there at that time was Mort Kaer, who was the first All-American from Southern Cal. He was our quarterback and I was at end. We got some attention because we had such a good team my senior year [1926]. Kaer was the best known of our players, and as a result a number of pro scouts came out to talk with us.

WEINMEISTER at Washington

I was born in Canada, in a little town named Rhein, about forty miles from Regina, Saskatchewan, but we moved to the United States when I was six months old. I was raised in Portland, Oregon.

When I was finishing up high school we moved to Seattle. There were several colleges that offered me scholarships; University of Oregon was the only one I considered besides Washington, which was my first choice. But I guess I had really predetermined that I was going to go to the U. of Washington right there in Seattle.

I started out playing end there as a sophomore in 1942 and then went into the service. When I got out in 1946 I came back and started as a fullback but got my knee wrecked. As a senior I switched to tackle and, of course, we played both ways in those days.

While I was still playing fullback, the New York Yankees of the All-America Football Conference sent a man over to talk to me. They were training over in Spokane then. They told me they had me as their first choice in their draft. So they sent me a contract right off, apparently to prevent anyone else from signing me. They offered me what was at that time a pretty good salary. I didn't talk with anyone from the NFL. So I signed with the Yankees.

The Yankees coach, Ray Flaherty, invited me to come over to Gonzaga, a college in Spokane, where the Yankees were training. They were having an exhibition game that evening, and I saw the players sitting out in front of the gym there at Gonzaga before they went into the locker room to get dressed. I thought, gee, these guys are really fat. But the most amazing thing to me in watching the game that night was to see how quick and fast they were. That was an eye-opener for me.

LYNCH at Notre Dame

I was born in New York, went through my first six grades in Manhasset, out on Long Island, while we were living in the Great Neck–Roslyn area. Then we moved out to Patenburg, New Jersey, and lived on a farm. I went to Phillipsburg Catholic High School, which was in a town right across the river from Easton, Pennsylvania.

I was a halfback at Phillipsburg. Our coach there, Charlie Passini, wrote a letter to Frank Leahy at Notre Dame when I was a senior, which said something to the effect that I've got a kid here I think can play for your team. Leahy sent the letter on to a scout whose name was McGinley, a postman in the area; and he, unbe-

Dick Lynch corrals the ever-elusive Jim Brown in a 1963 game, but the Giants sustained one of their three losses for the year that day against Cleveland, 35-24. Lynch was a mainstay in the Giants' defensive backfield from 1959 through 1966. No. 13 of the Browns is quarterback Frank Ryan.

knownst to me, scouted me. Then one day he just walked in and said, "We'd like to offer you a scholarship to Notre Dame."

Aubrey Lewis, who was from Montclair, New Jersey, and I were invited to come over to meet Frank Leahy in Newark after that. We shook his hand, and all he said, essentially, was, "Kids, do you want to come to Notre Dame?" We said, "Yes, sir," and that was it. We didn't sign any papers or anything like that. He felt a handshake was all that was necessary. That was the way he handled things—his word, your word; you understood the deal, sealed with a handshake.

I never played for Frank Leahy. The spring before I got there he resigned, and Terry Brennan took over for the 1954 season. I played halfback on offense and right cornerback on defense for Brennan. Terry was an excellent coach, and he had a great staff: Hank Stram, who later won a Super Bowl; Bill Walsh [not to be confused with the Bill Walsh who coached the San Francisco 49ers to four Super Bowl victories], who was one of the best offensive line coaches ever to coach in college and the NFL; Bill Fischer, an All-American guard when he played at Notre Dame, who coached the defensive line; and Jim Finks, who coached the quarterbacks for a year or two.

The biggest game I was ever in at Notre Dame was in 1957, my senior year. We went down to Norman to play Oklahoma. They had a forty-seven-game winning streak at the time, the longest ever in the NCAA—it still is the record, in fact. They had beat us the year before 40–0 in South Bend. They were an eighteen-point favorite. We didn't care. In '57 we were really prepared for them. We worked our asses off the week before the game. Terry Brennan kept reminding us that we were the last team to have defeated Oklahoma, which was all the way back in 1953 [it was the opening game of the season at Oklahoma, and Notre Dame prevailed 28–21].

We decided we were going to book-end their winning streak. Our defense was outstanding that day—just shut them down completely. In the fourth quarter it was 0–0. Then we marched eighty yards down the field. Bobby Williams called all the plays from the huddle, and we just surged. We were at the 3-yard line with a fourth down and a little less than four minutes to go. We decided to go for the touchdown. They were all scrunched up in the middle, thinking we were going to give the ball to our fullback, Nick Pietrosante, who, after all, was an All-American. Bob Williams faked the ball to him and Nick hit the line, and then Bob pitched the ball out to me and I went around right end, untouched, for the score. Monty Stickles kicked the extra point and we won 7–0. As we later learned, Oklahoma had not been shut out in 123 consecutive games. That was a great day, the highlight of my college football career.

Paul Hornung was the big guy at Notre Dame my sophomore and junior years. He had a buddy down there who was another halfback, Sherrill Sipes. I used to tell him "Paul, Sipes walks on eggs. Don't give him the ball. Give me the ball." Paul said I was the cockiest ballplayer he ever met. We never saw much of Paul around school. He must have graduated from St. Joseph's or someplace else. The only time we saw him was in the huddle.

SIMMS at Morehead State

I didn't choose Morehead State [Morehead, Kentucky], it chose me. I was from Kentucky and it was the only full scholarship offer for football I had.

There are a lot of memories attached to it. We played many, many games in very sparse surroundings. Some fields were definitely not even of college caliber. We'd travel all night on a bus to go play a game against teams like Eastern

Phil Simms, coming out of tiny Morehead State College, quarterbacked the Giants from 1979 through 1993 and virtually rewrote the passing chapter of the club's record book. When his career ended after the '93 season, he had thrown more passes (4,647), completed more passes (2,576), gained more yards passing (33,462), and tossed for more touchdowns (199) than any Giant in history.

Kentucky, our biggest rival, and others in our conference like East Tennessee State, Tennesse Tech, Murray State, and some at-large teams who wanted to book us to beat us. I always tell people, "Hey, when we went on the road, it was always a homecoming. We were everyone's homecoming guest." One of the good things about those at-large games, at least we got to play in front of a lot of people. At home, we didn't have very big crowds, maybe a couple thousand people at best.

NEWMAN at Michigan

It was actually Benny Friedman who was most instrumental in getting me to go to Michigan and play football. He had been a great quarterback there in the 1920s, and when I was a senior [in high school] he was already established as the best passer in the NFL.

Benny had a summer camp out in New Hampshire, and a lot of kids from Detroit and Cleveland went to it. I was one of them. It wasn't a football camp like

Harry Newman took over as quarterback for the Giants in 1933 and guided the offense the next three years. An excellent passer and runner, he led the league in completions, passing yardage, and passing touchdowns and was the team's top rusher during his rookie year. Newman led the Giants to a divisional title that season and to an NFL championship the following year.

they have these days—just an ordinary summer camp. Benny was the head counselor. He was a very nice guy and took an interest in me. He thought I would have a good college football career and told me I would be better off at Michigan than anywhere else. And it was Benny who taught me how to pass. We worked on it a lot. I think I may have thrown two passes in high school and that was all. Benny felt if I was going to make it to the top in college I needed to be a good passer as well as a runner. And, of course, he was right. Later on, Benny stopped working at that summer camp in New Hampshire, and I got the job as head counselor.

So I enrolled at Michigan and began playing football there my freshman year. We had some mighty good football players the years that I was at Michigan, quite a number of All-Americans. We had the first of the Wistert brothers, but he didn't go on to play pro football like his brother Al did later on. Bill Hewitt was a fine end and, of course, he had a terrific pro career with the Chicago Bears and Philadelphia Eagles and was put in the Pro Football Hall of Fame. Ivy Williamson went on to become a coach and athletic director at Wisconsin. In my sophomore year, there was a center and linebacker by the name of Doc Morrison, who made All-American; he played a couple of years with the Brooklyn Dodgers. In my junior and senior years our center was Chuck Bernard, and he was an All-American, too; he later played for the Detroit Lions.

I had been what they called a "junior All-American" in my sophomore year [1930] at Michigan—had a real fine year. But as a junior I broke an ankle, and I played most of the year with it until we found out it was in fact broken. It slowed me down a lot that year.

In my senior year we earned a share of the national championship [Michigan, with a record of 8–0–0, shared the title with Southern Cal, 10–0–0]. We also won the Big Ten title that year. We beat Northwestern, who used to have great teams around that time. They had Pug Rentner, an All-American halfback—and he was very good in the pros too, with the Boston Redskins.

My ankle was fine my senior year, and I had a great season. A lot of our games were close—and the last one was really a tough one. It was up in Minnesota and the temperature was six degrees below zero. They had Biggie Munn then, who would become a great coach, and Jack Manders, who was a fine back and kicker and would later play for the Bears—"Automatic Jack" they used to call him, because he was such a consistently good kicker. We just barely got by them to save our perfect record. I kicked a field goal, and that was the only score of the game.

I was named to the All-America team, and that meant an awful lot to me. I also won the Douglas Fairbanks Trophy that year, which was sort of like the Heisman Trophy. The Heisman didn't come along until a few years later [1936]. And I was given the *Chicago Tribune* trophy for most valuable player in the Big Ten.

Actually, we lost only one game in the three years I played at Michigan. In my sophomore year, we won eight games and were tied once. Then in my junior year—that was the year I had the bad ankle—we lost once to Ohio State. They had Sid Gillman that year, who went on to become a famous coach in the NFL. The only reason we lost it was because Jack Heston, one of our key running backs, got hammered on the opening kickoff. Jack was the son of Willie Heston, one of the all-time great football players at Michigan who played for Fielding Yost back in the early 1900s. Anyway, Jack was totally stunned—he was really unconscious—but he functioned, and we didn't know his condition until later. So he stayed in the game. But he fumbled the ball three times, each somewhere around our 20-yard line. On two of them they scored afterwards. That's really why they beat us. I wasn't able to play the entire game either because my ankle was bothering me too much. But that was really something—only one loss in three years, and we played many of the very best teams in the nation.

> **"I broke an ankle, and I played most of the year with it until we found out it was in fact broken. It slowed me down a lot that year."**
> **–HARRY NEWMAN**

2
Joining the Giants

DON CHANDLER and
SAM HUFF, 1956

It isn't pretty down there on the field, as reflected in this portrait of the Giants' Sam Huff. The great middle linebacker toiled in the trenches for the Giants from 1956 through 1963. He was elected to the Pro Football Hall of Fame in 1982.

One of the most often told tales among Giants nostalgics concerns a pair of twenty-one-year-old disheartened rookies in 1956—linebacker Sam Huff and punter Don Chandler, whose professional careers almost ended before they even began.

Huff, a third-round draft choice, and Chandler, a fifth-rounder, were not happy with the way things were going at the Giants' training camp up at St. Michael's College in Winooski, Vermont. Huff had played tackle at West Virginia, but, at 6'1" and 230 pounds, he was considered too small for that position in the pros. The rumor that a few of the coaches thought he was too slow for any other position got back to him, and he was, in his words, "disheartened, miserable, and homesick." Chandler was suffering from an injured shoulder and not doing well in camp and therefore was often the butt of Jim Lee Howell's "bellering," as the players called the coach's remonstrations.

One day after workouts, the two decided it was hopeless and that they might as well go home. Line coach Ed Kolman heard about the situation and cornered Huff. "You'll never forgive yourself if you leave now," he told him. "You'll feel like a quitter."

Huff shook his head. "It's not working out. I'm just wasting my time here."

"I've seen some great ones," Kolman said. "And I think if you stick it out you could be one of them in a few years. You've got talent, and I mean it. Don't throw it away by leaving."

The vote of confidence was enough to persuade Huff to stay, but when the linebacker tried to talk Chandler out of departing, he couldn't. So Huff agreed to accompany his friend to the airport in Burlington, Vermont. What happened there is described by Don Smith, former publicity chief of the Giants, in a book he wrote in 1960.

There they were informed that Chandler's flight would be late. It might be an hour or more before he could leave. The players drifted into the hot waiting room and plopped down on a bench. As the minutes ticked by, Huff began to wonder if he had made the right decision; whether or not he should get his bags and join Chandler as they had originally planned. Despite Kolman's comforting words, Sam was losing his confidence again.

Just then a station wagon roared up to the terminal and out bolted [then Giants assistant coach Vince] Lombardi. He dashed through the waiting room and pursued Chandler almost to the revved-up plane, which had just taxied up to the passenger gate.

"Hold on," Lombardi shouted in a voice that was disturbingly familiar to all Giant rookies. "You may not make this ball club,

Don Chandler almost left the Giants before getting a chance to kick a single football, but the disillusioned kicker was brought back into the fold by assistant coach Vince Lombardi during summer camp in 1956. Chandler placekicked and punted for the Giants until 1965, when he was traded to the Green Bay Packers and reunited with Lombardi. He still holds the Giants' record for the most PATs in a season, 52, and the "Babe," as he was called by some, has the standard for punting-average during a career, 43.8 yards, and in a single season, 46.6 in 1959.

Chandler, but you're sure as hell not quitting on me now. And neither are you, Huff, in case you've got any idea about running out." With that he packed the rookies into the station wagon and delivered them back to camp.

"If that plane had been on time," Huff recalls, "Chandler would have been on it. And maybe I would have gone with him."

ROSEY BROWN, 1953

I never even thought about playing professional football there [for the Giants]. In those days if you were black, you didn't do much thinking about playing for the pros at all. There were only a few in the league. Some teams didn't have any. The Redskins didn't sign a black until the 1960s. There were a few around at that time: Marion Motley, Bill Willis, Tank Younger, Deacon Dan Towler, Len Ford, and, of course, Emlen Tunnell, who was with the Giants—he'd joined them in 1948, the first black they ever hired. He was a walk-on—came to see Wellington Mara and got himself a job.

So I was very surprised when I learned I was drafted by the Giants. In fact, I didn't even know anything about the Giants then. I got a letter from the Giants and then Em Tunnell came down and told me about being drafted, what it meant and everything. The way I saw it, I was chosen to play for the Giants, just like I was chosen to play for Morgan State. I had no idea they could cut you.

They sent me a contract for—I think it was—$2,700 a year [$225 per regular season game]. I showed it to my coach at Morgan, Eddie Hurt, and he said, "Sign it. That's more than I got when I started teaching and coaching." Then I just signed it and sent it back.

DICK MODZELEWSKI, 1956

A lot of things developed there that year in Pittsburgh. I thought the world of Art Rooney, the Steelers' owner, but I had some other problems with the team. During the year, my wife was going to have a baby, and I went in to see [coach Walt] Kiesling and asked if I could go home—she was due with our first kid any day. He told me if I went it was going to cost me $500. At that time, it was a lot of dough—I was making maybe $7,000-something.

I thought about it and finally said, "Oh, go to hell," and got dressed and went home. As it was, I missed the delivery of the baby. Kiesling, as it turned out, didn't fine me—but only because Art Rooney told him not to. When my next year's contract came up, I didn't have any heart for it. I told them I wanted a million dollars, that's what it would take to get me to come back and play for Kiesling—otherwise, trade me.

They took me up on it. It was a convoluted deal: I was traded to the Lions, and they sent me to the Giants. I was with Detroit for two days, and they sent me to New York for Ray Krouse, who had played for my alma mater, Maryland, and had been with the Giants since 1951. I remember getting a call from Wellington Mara after the deal sending me to Detroit, and he said something like, "Don't get too comfortable there." Well, moving on to the Giants was the best thing that ever happened to me in pro football.

I had to report to St. Michael's in Winooski, Vermont, where the Giants were holding training camp in 1956. I met up with Andy Robustelli, Jim Katcavage, Sam Huff, and Rosey Grier. Most of us were new to the Giants that year except for Grier, but after about two weeks I said to my wife, "This is a winning ball club. I can just tell." We really melded into a family.

It was very different from the Steelers. Jack Mara, who was running the operation then, the coaches, and the veteran players all made you feel welcome, that you were a real part of the team. And in training camp we were out there in shorts and baseball caps in the morning, pads in the afternoon. During the season we never wore pads at practice. And consequently we did not get beat to hell by our own team as we had in Pittsburgh.

ANDY ROBUSTELLI, 1956

I was traded to the Giants in 1956. Sid Gillman, who had taken over as the Rams' head coach in 1955, decided to shake things up because of the championship-game loss that year. A number of the players were traded away. Besides me, Big Daddy Lipscomb and Ed Hughes from the defensive unit were dealt away too.

Andy Robustelli came to the Giants in 1956 after five fine years with the Rams. For the next nine years, the comparatively small defensive end (6'0", 230 pounds) proved to be one of the greatest defensive players in Giants history. A five-time All-Pro during his years in New York, Robustelli was elected to the Pro Football Hall of Fame in 1971.

What happened in my case was that I would ordinarily go home after the season was over, back to Connecticut. Well, in those days guys would straggle into training camp—it wasn't as regimented as it is today. But in 1956, Sid said we all had to be there at the very start, to get going, so we could wipe out the defeat we'd suffered in the title game of '55.

We talked by telephone before camp and I said to him, "Coach, I can't. I need a couple extra days. We're going to have another child any day, and I need to be here for that and be sure everything's okay."

He said, "No, you're coming out here or I'm getting rid of you."

I said, "Well, if you're going to do that, okay, but I'm not going to be there." And the next day he traded me to the Giants.

The Giants were a great contrast to the Rams—a completely different organization. The Rams were glitzy, Hollywood style—everything was kind of show business. The Giants were more the hard-nosed football team, and that entire conference was that way. The attitude was hard-nosed on all levels. The ballplayers did not get pampered as they did in Los Angeles or with the 49ers out on the coast. You got your own socks and your own jocks; you did everything yourself whereas with the Rams everything was sort of laid out for you. It was quite a difference.

It really was the best thing that could have happened to me, however, to come home to New York. I could live at home in Connecticut and commute. We still weren't making much money—this was my sixth year in the NFL and I think I was earning $7,500.

FRANK GIFFORD, 1952

I was, I have to admit, surprised when I ended up with the Giants in the 1952 draft. Before it, I had been contacted by the Los Angeles Rams and was under the impression they were going to take me. At the time I knew one of the minority owners, and he had told me that the Rams were seriously considering taking me in the first round.

The Rams drew the bonus pick that year, which gave them the very first choice in the draft, but they didn't take me. Instead they selected Bill Wade, a quarterback from Vanderbilt. The Giants took me somewhere farther down the line in the first round.

I was a little teed off about the whole situation and even considered not playing, and that thought got even stronger when the Giants offered me my first contract. I was making more money working part-time in the studios in Hollywood

With credentials from Southern Cal and Hollywood good looks, Frank Gifford became one of the most recognizable Giants of all time. He was instrumental in bringing the team to five NFL title games in the 1950s and early '60s. He was named All-Pro four times and went to seven Pro Bowls during his twelve-year career with the Giants.

in bit parts as an extra and a stuntman. I'd been offered several thousand more dollars for a full-time job with a studio than the Giants were putting up for me to play professional football. I was also offered more money to play for Edmonton in the Canadian Football League.

I guess I was just miffed at being misled by the Rams. At the same time I'd gotten married in college and we had a baby, and so naturally I was concerned about what I'd be earning and also the security. The first contract the Giants offered me was, I believe, for $7,500. Edmonton had offered me $10,000.

At any rate, Mel Hein, the Giants' great center of the 1930s and early 1940s, was one of our assistant coaches at USC—the line coach—and he told me about what a fine organization the Giants were and how much he liked and respected the Maras. Then I got a call from Wellington Mara, congratulating me and saying they would shortly be sending me a contract. I didn't even ask about the money at that time.

When I got the contract, I called Wellington Mara and told him I couldn't do it for $7,500. We talked a couple of times and I wound up finally signing for—I think it was—$8,000 and a $250 signing bonus.

MEL HEIN, 1931

I went from Washington State to the New York Giants, but I almost went with another team. Portsmouth [the Spartans], out in Ohio, was in the league then— that was before the team moved the franchise to Detroit and became the Lions. They wanted me, and I had a contract offer from them. I had another contract offer from the Providence Steam Roller, out of New England, who were also in the league at that time, and it was better than the one from Portsmouth. I hadn't received anything from the Giants, although I'd heard they were planning to make me an offer. Well, Jimmy Conzelman, the Steam Roller coach, was pushing me, so I signed with Providence for $125 a game, which was a pretty good salary for a lineman in those days. When I started in 1931 a lot of the linemen were only making $80 or $85 a game.

After I signed the contract, I went down to Spokane for a basketball game, another sport I played at Washington State. We were playing Gonzaga, and Ray Flaherty, the captain of the Giants at that time, was coaching [basketball] there during the off season. He came down to the dressing room after the game and asked me if I'd received a contract from the Giants yet.

"No, I haven't," I said. "But if one is on the way, it's too late now." Ray didn't know what I was talking about, so I told him. "I signed one with the

Providence Steam Roller and mailed it back to them yesterday."

Ray said, "Oh, no. How much are they paying you?"

I told him and he said, "The Giants' contract is a better offer, $150 a game. I know that's the figure, and I know the contract's on its way to you. Damn!" A little later he came back to me and said, "Why don't you go down to the postmaster when you get home and ask him to send a telegram to the postmaster in Providence to see if he would intercept the letter?"

The next morning I went down there, but the postmaster said he wouldn't do it. He said that I could try myself but that he truly doubted I'd get the letter back. So I sent a telegram myself, and, sure enough, the letter with the contract came back, and in the meantime the contract from the Giants for $150 a game had arrived. I signed with the Giants and tore up the other contract with Providence. I think at that time $150 was probably the highest pay of any lineman in the league. It was pretty good money, even though it would not sound that way now, but you could buy a loaf of bread for a nickel and get a full meal for thirty-five cents in the Automat back then. And you had no income tax.

Mel Hein (No. 7) shows a little of his defensive skills here, converging on an unidentified ball-carrier. An outstanding linebacker for the Giants throughout the 1930s and early '40s, he was also recognized on offense as the finest center the game had seen up to that time in NFL history.

NEW MAN IN TOWN

New York sportswriters John Kieran and later Barry Gottherer wrote of the arrival of Shipwreck Kelly at the Giants in 1932 and his departure later that same season.

It was in the summer that a big, lanky, redheaded chap came into Tim Mara's office on Twenty-third Street.

"Ah'm Shipwreck Kelly," explained the visitor.

"What?" said Mr. Mara. "The fellow who sits on flagpoles?"

"No, suh," said the visitor. "Ah play football. Played foh Kaintucky."

Mara, who had been given a list of the top college prospects by his sixteen-year-old son Wellington, suddenly realized who his visitor was. "Welcome," said the Giants' owner, smiling and offering a chair. "I've heard of you, my boy. Here, look at this." Opening his drawer, Mara pulled out a folder crammed with clippings detailing the exploits of Shipwreck Kelly of Kentucky.

"I've seen them all," said Kelly, "and I'd lak to play football this fall with yah Giants. Ah hear it's a right smart team, suh."

Mara and the Giants needed Kelly, but not at his price—a percentage of the gate similar to the deal Red Grange had [with the Chicago Bears] back in 1925. "I'd love to have you, but I can't afford you," said Mara. "Well, the news about the Depression will get back to the hills of Kentucky sooner or later, and you might as well be the one to carry the word."

The Giants had not heard the last of Shipwreck Kelly.

Totally unannounced, the drawling, redheaded halfback reported to the Giants training camp at Magnetic Springs, Ohio.

"Glad to have you," said [coach Steve] Owen, "but really we weren't expecting you."

"That's why I came," drawled Kelly. "I do the most astonishing things. Nevah know why myself. Now, coach, there's nothin' to do but give me the ball and let me get going."

ARNIE WEINMEISTER, 1950

When the All-America Conference folded after the 1949 season, the Giants got a kind of special deal. In exchange for allowing Ted Collins to keep the New York Bulldogs [which was an NFL franchise that had been allowed to come down from Boston the year before and which later became the New York Yanks in 1950] in New York, the Giants got to select six players from the now defunct Brooklyn/New York Yankees of the AAFC.

The Giants took me and a couple of terrific defensive backs—Tom Landry and Otto Schnellbacher. So I joined the NFL in 1950.

When the Giants selected me, they sent me a letter that said something to the effect that they were happy to have me and that they were proud to offer me a contract. Only thing was, the contract offered $6,400 for the year. The year before, with the Yankees, I'd made $10,000. So I wrote back and I told them that I wasn't interested because I wouldn't play for any less than I had the year before. The banter went back and forth over phone calls for some time.

Meanwhile, I had gone back to Seattle and the Giants were in training camp. By this time I'd gone to work for the Aetna Life Insurance Company. The Giants

Arnie Weinmeister takes on two white-shirted Giants' blockers in a practice session during the early 1950s. An All-Pro tackle in each of his four years with the Giants (1950-53), Weinmeister was considered as fast as most of the backs in the NFL despite his more than 250-pound weight.

called again and said they really wanted me to come back and talk contract. I said I would if they provided me a first-class, round-trip airline ticket. They did.

The Giants were in training up at Saranac Lake, New York. So I went up there. It was around lunchtime when I arrived, and they suggested I go have lunch with the players and that we would get together afterwards. So I set my bag in the hall of the lodge there, which is called the Eagle's Nest, and had lunch. A couple of former teammates with the Yankees, Tom Landry and Otto Schnellbacher, were sitting with me, and they were telling me that they were badly in need of tackles. That reinforced my resolve for the upcoming meeting.

I met with Wellington Mara and the coach, who was Steve Owen at the time—the only coach they'd had over the previous twenty years. I told them that under no circumstances would I play for any less than $10,000 the first year, $11,000 the second, and a two-year, no-cut contract. A no-cut contract in those days was unheard of.

They said they simply weren't going to do that.

I said, "Well, that's fine. I haven't even unpacked my bag, and so I'll be on my way." And I got up.

They said, reluctantly, "Okay, we'll write up the contract."

Phil Simms tries to unleash a pass over the ferocious rush of Chicago Bear defensive end Richard Dent in a game between two of the premier teams of the mid-1980s. Simms led the Giants to two NFL championships (1986 and 1990) and was heralded as the MVP of Super Bowl XXI.

PHIL SIMMS, 1979

When the announcement was made during the 1979 NFL draft at New York's Waldorf Astoria Hotel that Phil Simms of tiny Morehead State was the Giant's first-round selection, it was greeted with a chorus of boos from the spectators.

I don't know if it's as bad as people think. It was actually a reenactment when the booing occurred. Pete Roselle was up there announcing it a second time for the television camera. The first time it sort of slipped by, but when he was on camera they booed. It was no great surprise to me. I remember thinking while I was down there in Morehead, Kentucky, after I learned the Giants were going to draft me, "Boy, I bet those people in New York are going to be a little upset when they hear my name."

I wasn't all that happy about it, either. I learned about it from my coach. The Giants were calling him all the time for information about me. I didn't think it was true at first, but he said "Phil, I'm telling you, there is no question, you are going to be drafted by the Giants with the seventh pick in the first round." I didn't even think about it in the terms you would now. I wasn't thinking, "Well, if I go seventh, that's a big contract." All I was thinking was which teams I would rather play for: the Green Bay Packers, the Kansas City Chiefs, San Diego, San Francisco, all of whom had expressed some interest in me, and all of whom were higher up on my list of who I'd like to play for than the Giants. At the time, I just thought, "Oh, I don't want to go to New York . . . Who wants to go to New York?" But once you experience it, I learned, it's a whole different feeling. Now I'm happy it's my home.

DICK LYNCH, 1959

The Redskins drafted me in 1958, and I didn't want to go there. It's a kind of story in itself. While I was at Notre Dame I joined the ROTC to get some pocket money. And I got very high grades in ROTC, a lot higher than the 83 [percent] or something I got in regular classes. After graduation you had to put down your preference; I preferred to serve six months, so I put that down.

I had no ambition at all to play pro football. I was going to take a job with Encyclopaedia Britannica in Chicago. After I signed up with EB for the job, I got a letter from the army saying I was drafted. I was to go in January of 1959 for two years. So I had to tell the people at Encyclopaedia Britannica I couldn't take the job.

At any rate, I was in Chicago to play in the College All-Star Game and I was interviewed on television. The guy asked me, "Dick, what are your plans for the future?"

"My plans have been drastically changed. I went to Notre Dame for four years and got a great education, and now I just found out I'm going to be stuck in the army for two years. I applied for six months but they stuck me for two years. I can't take the job I want. So, as long as I don't have to go in until January, maybe I'll try to play pro football until then."

So I went to the Redskins' training camp and I made the team. When we were back in Washington, I told George Preston Marshall, the team owner, about my two-year army commitment. He groused around and then tried to see if there was anything he could do, but there wasn't.

Well, as it turned out, some colonel had heard what I said on television and raised holy hell. He called Notre Dame and ranted about my saying I was going to be "stuck" in the army: "What kind of people are they turning out of ROTC

Dick Lynch (No. 22) leaps to block a St. Louis Cardinals' field goal attempt that has just left the toe of Gerry Perry. The Giants squeaked by, 31–28, one of the conquests in New York's nine-game winning streak that closed out the 1962 season and earned them the NFL East title. No. 20 for the Giants is Jim Patton, and No. 82 is Tom Scott.

down there? We don't want guys like him for two years!" and on and on. So I ended up getting the six months after all and served it at Fort Monmouth, New Jersey, after the first season with Washington.

I hadn't really been very happy with the Redskins, and I didn't plan to go back when I got out of the army. They sent me a couple of different contracts and I never sent one back. They got upset and finally just traded me to the Giants.

Everything then worked out. I liked the Giants and the Maras. Timmy Mara, whose family owned half the team, was a real good friend, and his uncle Wellington Mara, who owned the other half, was a fine man. And I knew the city real well. Tom Landry, who was coaching the defense then, was sensational to play for. Nobody could analyze an offense like he could. He'd tell you this is what's going to happen, and sure as hell it would. He told me when I got there that they definitely needed help at the right corner spot. They'd gotten beat the year before in the title game with Baltimore. The Colts and especially Raymond Berry had burned them a couple of times at the right corner.

I got the starting job, and we had a heckuva defensive backfield with Jimmy Patton, Dick Nolan, and Lindon Crow, and then Erich Barnes came in 1961—"The Baby," we used to call him. Erich and I, the "twin corners" they called us, were and are great pals.

The team was a very close-knit one when I came in 1959. There were some great ballplayers but no big egos. It was all a matter of working together as a team. Both units were that way—good camaraderie, respect for each other, no bullshit, stick up for each other, and we had a helluva lot of fun at the same time. I roomed with Cliff Livingston—we were both bachelors and lived in the Manhattan Hotel. We used to go over to Downey's all the time where a lot of the young actors in New York hung out, guys like John Cassavetes and Ben Gazzara who were just getting started in the theater.

PAT SUMMERALL, 1958

I was orginally with the Chicago Cardinals. By 1958 I was contemplating getting out of the game altogether. It was such a depressing situation, such a miserable operation there in Chicago. After the 1957 season, Pop Ivy replaced Ray Richards as head coach, and in the spring of 1958 I called Pop and asked if he wanted me back and, if so, what he had planned for me, where I would fit in—that kind of thing. He told me, "You're a key part of the team, a key part of the operation. Yes! We want you back."

About a week later, I was over at the post office down where I lived in Lake City, and I picked up the afternoon paper and saw that I had been traded to the Giants.

I called Jim Lee Howell, who was the Giants' head coach at the time. I knew him from Arkansas—he went there, too. He was the athletic-dorm supervisor when I was there. He was in graduate school, and his job was to keep the young guys in line. I asked him what his plans for me were, and he told me that he wanted a kicker who could also play. They had Ben Agajanian at the time, who was getting up there in years and just wanted to come in on the weekends to kick in the game and stay home the rest of the week. So I asked him what weight he wanted me to come in at, and he said around 230, which is what I was [Summerall was 6'4"].

I became their kicker, played on most of the special teams, and was the third defensive end behind Andy Robustelli and Jim Katcavage.

HARRY NEWMAN, 1933

After I got out of college, I had several offers to go with the pros. I wasn't very big, and that was a drawback. I was only about 175 pounds in college, and I was only 5'8". But George Halas of the Chicago Bears came up with an offer. It wasn't a very good one. The New York Giants came up with a better one. I talked with Tim Mara and I got the feeling they really wanted a passer and that I'd fit in with them right away.

The contract deal he came up with was that I was actually to receive a percentage of the gate. That was a very good deal in those days. As I remember it, the first year I was supposed to get 10 percent of the gate after $11,000 had been deducted for expenses. The second year I was to get 20 percent.

It was kind of a foregone conclusion, I guess, that I was to be the starting quarterback—or tailback, I think you'd call it. So I really wasn't treated like a rookie when I showed up there. We had our training camp at Pompton Lakes over in New Jersey back then. And from the time I got there I was starting. We had two sessions each day at camp, and I think that was the first time they started that; but it was turning into a different kind of game with all the passing we were going to do— a lot of new plays and all that.

ALEX WEBSTER, 1955

Al DeRogatis, who at one time had been an outstanding defensive tackle for the Giants and was now a scout for the team, had come up to watch us in 1954. He was looking basically at Sam Etcheverry, a quarterback, and he came back to New York with my name. Wellington Mara then offered me a contract, and I took it. It was for $10,000 with a $2,500 signing bonus. Up in Canada, even though I'd gotten the MVP award the year before, the offer was only $5,500. So I became a Giant.

After I signed with the Giants, Montreal came back and offered me more than the Giants were going to pay me, but I told them I wouldn't do it.

New York certainly offered one advantage: I could commute during the season from New Jersey, where my family was living, to the Polo Grounds, where we were practicing and playing. We were just across the Hudson River from Manhattan. In Canada, I didn't earn enough to bring my family up there, and that made life less than pleasant.

The Giants in 1955, when I arrived, were just coming into their own. Jim Lee Howell had taken over from Steve Owen and instituted a more modern

Game action, 1956. Quarterback Don Heinrich hands off to fullback Mel Triplett in a game against the Pittsburgh Steelers.

The Bald Eagle, as Y. A. Tittle was appropriately nicknamed, he warms up before a game during the 1963 season. Tittle, at the age of thirty-four, came to the Giants in 1961 after an illustrious career with the Baltimore Colts (1948–50) and the San Francisco 49ers (1951–60). He quarterbacked the Giants for four years, leading them to the NFL title game in 1963, before retiring after the '64 season, acknowledged as one of the game's finest passing quarterbacks ever. He was inducted into the Pro Football Hall of Fame in 1971.

game. He had Lombardi and Landry on his coaching staff; he had a lot of very good ballplayers who were coming into their own.

Y. A. TITTLE, 1961

I was going into my fourteenth season in 1961 when the 49ers decided to trade me to the Giants. I had very mixed feelings about it. I didn't know whether to retire or not to retire. One of the reasons I was thinking about retiring was because in the 1960 season I had a groin pull that bothered me from about the fourth game on and it seemed I never could get well. I'd lay off a game and then I'd come back, and it would come back. So I had a miserable season.

Back then Red Hickey, our coach, was using the shotgun offense exclusively—not just occasionally like teams do today, but on every play. The quarterback was like a tailback in the old single-wing offense. It was more suited to the talents of John Brodie, who was more mobile than I was. So with the switch to that, I thought there was a good chance I'd be traded; and, of course, I was.

I went up to the Giants' training camp in '61, which was held in Salem, Oregon, back then, and I still had the groin pull. It bothered me and I was concerned about it. I didn't want to tell the trainers about it. In fact, I would actually go into the toilet and tape myself so they wouldn't find out about it. I'd flush the toilet while I was tearing the tape so no one would hear it. Then I'd get the tape on and go out and get some practice.

They asked me to play in the first game that year, an exhibition game against the Rams down in Los Angeles. On the first play I was in for, I fumbled the snap from Ray Wietecha. Their linebacker—I think it was Jack Pardee—came down on me and his knee got me in the back, and I ended up with a couple of broken bones there. They took me out of the game after that play. I was out for six weeks.

During that healing time I'd get in the hot tub every day, and it healed my groin injury too.

Everything was fine after that. I moved to New York—didn't bring my wife, just got an apartment near Yankee Stadium for the season. I roomed there with Del Shofner, who had also come to the Giants on a trade—they got him from the Rams, and it was one of the Giants' best trades ever.

Charlie Conerly had been the starting quarterback for years when I got to New York—since 1948. We came into the pros the same year but Charlie was about three or so years older than me. He'd spent his whole career with the Giants. And Charlie was a fine gentleman; we became good friends. I'm sure he felt some pressure when they brought me in. We were both old—he was thirty-seven and I was thirty-four.

LAWRENCE TAYLOR, 1981

Lawrence Taylor's career in New York almost ended before it began when certain Giants threatened a walkout over his agent's salary demands in the days leading up to the 1981 NFL draft. The consensus All-American linebacker from North Carolina talked about it to the *New York Times*:

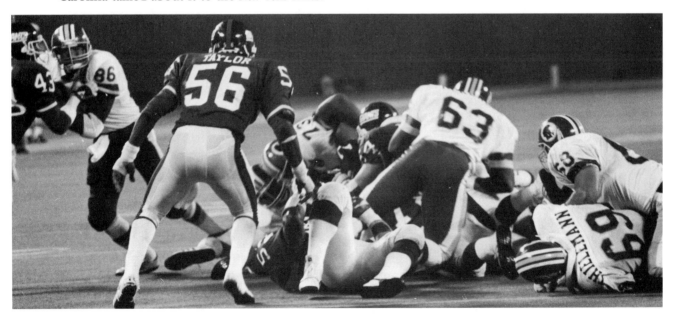

A rare moment: Lawrence Taylor (No. 56) is caught watching the action. The game is for the NFC championship of 1986, and Taylor along with the rest of the Giants defense held the Redskins scoreless that day, the final score 17-0. Taylor, regarded as perhaps the greatest outside linebacker ever to play the game, was enshrined in the Pro Football Hall of Fame in 1999.

"I'd heard the talk that some of the Giants would walk out if I got a lot of money," the North Carolina linebacker said. "I didn't want people to get mad at me. So I sent the Giants a telegram Monday saying I would rather not be drafted by them.

"Monday night I got calls from some of the players on the offense and the defense, and some of the coaches. They said there was nothing to the story, and there would be no walkout. They said they wanted me here. That made me feel better."

Taylor arrived in New York on April 28, 1981, the same day the draft began. He seemed to enjoy his initial exposure to the Big Apple. "I'll enjoy New York," he said. "You've got a pretty good selection of TV up here. I watched *The Three Stooges*. I like them." It would not be long before Taylor, clad in a Giants uniform number 56, began making opposing offensive linemen, quarterbacks, and running backs look like stooges themselves.

RED BADGRO, 1930

I was thinking mostly about playing professional baseball when my college days were over. And I had a couple of offers. I still had a couple of units to go at USC when one day I bumped into a fraternity brother who had also been a starter on our football team. He was leaving the frat house with a suitcase and told me he was going out east to join Red Grange's New York Yankees. He asked me if I wanted to play pro football. I told him I hadn't really thought about it because baseball was what I had in mind. I said I probably wouldn't mind playing it, however.

He said he would make a pitch for me when he got to New York. "You'll hear from me in a couple of days," he said. "That is, if they haven't signed up all their ends yet." And I got a call in a couple of days, and pretty soon I was on the train going from L.A. to New York.

The Yankees were owned by C. C. Pyle [the entrepreneur who arranged the famous Red Grange/Chicago Bears national barnstorming tour in 1925], and I think Grange had part of it as well. They had been in the league Pyle started, the first American Football League, the year before, 1926. When that league went broke and folded up, the Yankees were brought into the NFL. We were a road team for the most part [they played only three of their sixteen games in Yankee Stadium]. The Giants were there, already well established and playing at the Polo Grounds. We had a pretty good team. We had Grange, of course, but he got his knee pretty badly hurt after about four games. We also had Eddie Tryon, who was a good running back. He had been an All-American at Colgate. I got to start at one end and Ray Flaherty was at the other. We also had Mike Michalske, a great lineman, and Wild Bill Kelly, who was our passer.

The Yankees broke up after the 1928 season. When they did, many of the fellows went to Green Bay, some went to the Bears, and a few went to the Giants. I was playing baseball at the time too, with the St. Louis Browns, and I thought maybe I'd just concentrate on that. I felt if I could hit pretty well and really make it in baseball—well, that would take care of it. But I didn't hit the ball as well as I thought I would; I wasn't in the starting lineup. So after two years I decided I'd go back to football.

I qualified as a free agent. Steve Owen came down to Houston, where I was playing in the Texas League at the time, and asked if I'd like to come to the Giants. I said sure. And so I spent the next six years in New York with the Giants.

Tim Mara signed me to my first contract with the Giants. He was a good owner. I never had any trouble with him—or any owner, for that matter. I signed up to play for just so much and that was it. At that time, we didn't consider what the other fellow got. If he made $500 a game or $1,000 or only $2, we didn't care. But the money sure wasn't very good in those days. I got $150 a game when I first signed with the Giants. I didn't exactly get rich on that salary.

KYLE ROTE, 1951

I really didn't know much about pro football while I was in college. The only team I ever followed—and that was only on occasion—was the Detroit Lions, because Doak and his buddy Bobby Layne played for them. I didn't really even know how the draft worked. In those days they had a bonus pick—each team would draw from a hat and one would get the bonus, the first pick, regardless of where the team had ended up in the previous year's standings. Then it would go in order like today—the team with the worst record picking, then the next worst, and so on.

In February or March of 1951, they held the draft and Steve Owen picked the bonus out of the hat. It was quite a bonus for the Giants because

Kyle Rote, an All-American tailback from Southern Methodist University, signs his first pro contract with the Giants in 1951 under the pleased eyes of Wellington Mara. It signaled the beginning of an illustrious Giants career that would last through the 1961 season.

"I was
wondering
how in the
hell I would
ever make
this team."
—JIM KATCAVAGE

they had a 10–2–0 record the year before and otherwise would have picked way down the line. Well, they selected me with it.

They called after the pick and wanted to know if I'd be amenable to talking to them. Then Wellington Mara came down to Dallas, and we agreed to the terms of a contract. A while later I went up to New York for the formal signing, which was done at Toots Shor's restaurant.

When I first arrived I stayed in the Concourse Plaza Hotel, which was up in the Bronx about two blocks up the hill from Yankee Stadium. I was married, and my wife and my oldest son, who had been born on Christmas Day 1950, came up to New York with me. We stayed in the Concourse Plaza during the football season for several years, but in the off season we would always go back to San Antonio. It wasn't until 1958 that we stayed permanently in New York.

I'd met a couple of the Giants before going to that first training camp; but when you go there, you know, every rookie is scared to death. Most of the players were pretty nice—guys like Charlie Conerly and Al DeRogatis, I remember, went out of their way. Charlie and I were a little closer in that he and his wife were also living in the Concourse Plaza. Tom Landry and his wife were living there too. Most of the single guys lived in other hotels down closer to the action.

JIM KATCAVAGE, 1956

A couple of NFL teams had expressed some interest in me during my senior year at Dayton and later out at the East-West Shrine Game, which I played in after the season. One of the more interested was the Giants. Vince Lombardi, who was on the coaching staff of the Giants then, scouted me my junior year. He watched me in spring practice before my senior year. I remember my coach, Hugh Devore, calling me in and saying there's this guy here to see you—Vince Lombardi. Hell, I didn't know who he was then. I sat down with him and he gave me all that rigamarole about someday you might be a good football player and crap like that. But I was pleased they were interested. Coincidentally, Hugh Devore had been the head coach of the Green Bay Packers in 1953 before coming to Dayton, and he would go on to coach the Philadelphia Eagles the same year I went into the NFL.

Well, the Giants did draft me. When I got there, I found out they had traded and got Andy Robustelli, who was not just a defensive end like I was but had already made All-Pro with the Rams a couple of times. And they had Walt Yowarsky, who had been with the Giants a couple of years. I was wondering how

Leaving the field, two memorable Giant defenders: Jim Patton (No. 20), a mainstay in the secondary from 1955 through 1966, and end Jim Katcavage (No. 75), who held down one end of the defensive line from 1956 through 1968.

in the hell I would ever make this team. But I did, and I had the starting job by the first regular-season game.

CHARLIE CONERLY, 1948

During that year [1947] the Redskins, I guess, decided they didn't want me anymore, and so they traded the rights to the Giants. I think they got Howie Livingston, a halfback, for me. Wellington Mara, I remember, came down to see me and watched our last game of the '47 season.

So I saw I was going to New York, which wasn't all that bad. After all, the Redskins had Sammy Baugh at the time. And I also felt New York was the place to be if you were going to be playing professional sports.

There was the story, too, around that time about me and the Brooklyn Dodgers and Branch Rickey, who owned that team in the AAFC. They had drafted me—they had their own draft then and didn't care about the NFL's draft. They offered me some money—a little more than the Giants, as I recall—but they were a new team, and I just felt the Giants had been playing football, what, twenty-some-odd years, and that sure seemed like a safer place to go. They wrote it up in the papers that the Dodgers [football team] were going to give me a $40,000 bonus or some such. Well, if they were I might have taken it. That was a lot of money in those days. There was all this stuff in the papers about money—big money, $15,000 a year for so many years—but it was all talk. It was written up that Branch Rickey was offering a package like more than $100,000, but figures tend to get all messed up between what they were offering and what the newspapers said they were offering. There was a gentleman who was a baseball scout for their baseball team who came to visit me, but that was almost all the contact I'd had with them. At any rate, I felt I made the right decision signing on with the Giants.

TOM LANDRY, 1950

In 1950, in the All-America Football Conference, there was a Yankees team, owned by Dan Topping, who also owned the baseball Yankees. That team I had heard about. There were some ballplayers who had gone up from Texas to play for the Yankees in the AAFC: Jack Russell from Baylor, Martin Ruby from Texas A&M, Pete Layden from Texas; and Bruce Alford from TCU. We had heard about them. So it was just a natural for me to take on with the Yankees, which I did, in 1949. At the time, I didn't know anything about the Giants in New York and had never heard from them. So, I just said what the heck and signed with the Yankees.

I remember I started out playing offensive halfback for the Yankees, and back-up defensive back to Harmon Rowe. Then in the second game of the year Harmon got hurt and they put me at defensive right half. Well, we were playing the Cleveland Browns and I had to cover Mac Speedie that day, and he set an All-America Conference record for yardage on pass receptions. He turned me every way but loose. That's when I got the sudden message I had to learn how to key on offenses and know what they were going to do before they snapped the ball. It was quite an initiation.

Well, the AAFC went out of business after the '49 season. And the way the thing worked was that the Maras, the family who owned the Giants, had territorial rights to New York City in the NFL.

Dan Topping gave up his AAFC franchise and so our Yankees team was gone. There was another Yankees team the NFL allowed to be brought down from Boston, which was owned by the singer Kate Smith and her agent [Ted Collins]. But with the NFL territorial rights in the hands of the Giants, to keep them happy the Maras

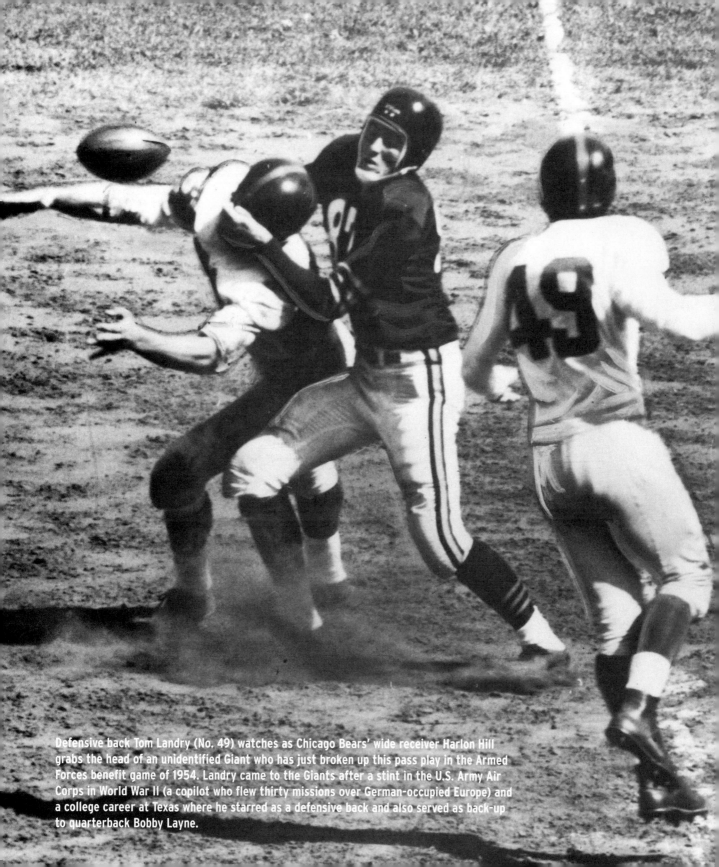

Defensive back Tom Landry (No. 49) watches as Chicago Bears' wide receiver Harlon Hill grabs the head of an unidentified Giant who has just broken up this pass play in the Armed Forces benefit game of 1954. Landry came to the Giants after a stint in the U.S. Army Air Corps in World War II (a copilot who flew thirty missions over German-occupied Europe) and a college career at Texas where he starred as a defensive back and also served as back-up to quarterback Bobby Layne.

were allowed to pick six or so players from Topping's Yankees. I remember they took almost all defensive players—Arnie Weinmeister, Otto Schnellbacher, Harmon Rowe, me. I think they took only one offensive player.

The Giants weren't nearly as flamboyant as the Yankees had been. The Giants were in an older league, well entrenched; you could just feel it. Topping's Yankees had been much more free-spirited in the way in which they were run. There was much more freedom in the upstart league. But you knew with the Giants this team was going to be around for a long, long time. It was an exceptionally well-run organization, and everyone inside was dedicated to making it work.

Sam Huff, 6'1", 230 pounds, was a two-way tackle at West Virginia. Drafted by the Giants in the third round in 1956, he was converted to middle linebacker by defensive coordinator Tom Landry during his rookie year. In the eight years he spent with the Giants, the team won six division titles and an NFL championship (1956), and Huff went to four Pro Bowls.

SAM HUFF, 1956

I was really surprised that the Giants drafted me. They were one of the few NFL teams I hadn't heard from. Almost all the others at least wrote me a letter, but not the Giants. So it surprised the hell out of me when they called and said they'd taken me in the third round [of the 1956 NFL draft].

Wellington Mara was the first to contact me. He called me down in West Virginia, told me about the draft, and said he wanted me to come up to New York. And he was the person I dealt with in regard to a contract. We didn't have agents in those days, so you had to handle the negotiations yourself; needless to say, the teams had the advantage.

When we met in New York, he said, "We'd like to sign you to a contract as soon as possible."

I said, "How much?"

"Seven thousand dollars," he said.

"That sounds good," I said, "but I promised Coach Lewis that I wouldn't sign any contract without consulting with him."

He said, "That's no problem. Why don't you call him from here?"

So I did. And Coach Lewis said, "They're going to pay you $7,000 for playing? That's like stealing. Wow, $7,000 for playing football! You sign that contract!"

I signed it, and then Wellington Mara asked me if I needed any money right then. And I said I did, I could really use $500 to pay off my furniture. So he wrote me a check. When I got my first paycheck, which was after the first regular-season game, the $500 was deducted. I thought it was a bonus, but I found it was an "advancement." They had signing bonuses back then, but I didn't get one. Gifford and Tittle got them, I believe.

The owners essentially knew what they could get away with in those days, and they took advantage of it—all of them did it; that's just the way it was. You even had to come to training camp with your own shoes. The team wouldn't buy any for you.

3 Game Time

The kick: Pat Summerall launches a forty-nine-yarder—some say a fifty-six-yarder—through a swirling snowstorm to give the Giants a 13–10 victory over the Cleveland Browns in 1958. It clinched a tie for the NFL East crown that year.

PAT SUMMERALL: The Fabled Field Goal, 1958

It is always a thrill to be put in a position where you can win a game for your team, although you don't think of it that way at the time. When the time comes to go into a situation like that—whether it's kicking a field goal, pinch-hitting, or shooting a free throw at the end of a game—you're totally oblivious to what's going on around you. It's almost like you're in a capsule. Everything around you is hazy; you aren't conscious that there are 70,000 people out there ready to cheer you or boo you. You don't hear any of that stuff. You just get yourself mentally ready to do what you have to do. I always tried to stay calm; I knew the more excited I got the less effective I'd be. Concentration is the key in a situation like that.

I had the chance, of course, to do it again in the last game of the season that year against the Browns, a game we had to win. They had it as a forty-nine-yarder. I don't really know how long it was because you couldn't see the yard markings.

Kyle Rote swears it was a fifty-six-yarder because he said he was standing on the sideline at the 50-yard line. All I remember about it is that when I got into the huddle, Charlie Conerly, my holder, looked at me and said, "What the fuck are you doing here?"

I said, "We're going to kick a field goal." He was in disbelief. But we did it, and it worked. I actually didn't see it go through the uprights—you couldn't see that far through the swirling snow. I could see the goalposts, but I couldn't see the ball. I knew when I kicked it I had the distance—you can just tell; like when you hit a golf shot square, you know it—but you don't know whether it might break to the right or the left. Fortunately it didn't.

The first person I saw when I came off the field was Lombardi, shaking his head. We were all jumping up and down, and Lombardi came up and said to me, "You know, you son of a bitch, you can't kick it that far." He had actually been against trying it, but Jim Lee Howell made the call.

TUFFY LEEMANS: The Giants vs. the Redskins, 1942

"We might as well take a chance now."
—TUFFY LEEMANS

We were playing the Redskins at Washington. We did not have a great football team because the war was on and we had some wartime ballplayers. Steve Owen said to me, "I don't want you to throw any passes. I don't want you to ever throw the ball in this game." I was the guy who called the plays from my halfback position.

Well, we come out for the game, and, Jesus, here over Griffith Stadium is the darkest cloud you've ever seen. You know from the looks of that cloud that the damn thing is going to let loose and rain all day. So on our first play from scrimmage I go into the huddle and say to our center, Mel Hein, and a few of the other old-timers, "Jesus, it's going to rain like hell. I think I'm going to fake a reverse to [halfback Ward] Cuff and run him wide and see what that Redskin halfback over there does. And if he does what I hope he will, then I'm going to pitch that ball to [end] Willie Walls."

"Jeez," Mel Hein says. "Don't start throwing. If they pick one off, Steve will blow his top."

"Mel," I say to him, "It's going to rain. We might as well take a chance now."

I told Walls to head straight down and to the outside. Then I ran Cuff wide on the fake, and this Redskin halfback, Steve Juzwick, comes barreling up there to stop Cuff. By the time Juzwick recovers, Walls is out there behind him. I throw the ball to Walls on the Washington 30-yard line, and he goes the rest of the way. It's

Tuffy Leemans, shown here carrying the ball against the Green Bay Packers, came to the Giants in 1936 after a teenage Wellington Mara went down to George Washington University and recruited him the year before. Proving Mara's sagacity, Leemans led the NFL in rushing with 830 yards as a rookie. Moving out to block for him here are Leland Shaffer (No. 20) and Dale Burnett (No. 18).

a fifty-yard touchdown play to put us ahead 7–0. And now it rains. It rains and it rains and it rains.

Washington scores in the second quarter to make it 7–7. Then in the third quarter one of our ends, Neal Adams, drops off on one of their flat passes and picks it off and goes sixty-five yards for a touchdown. We beat the Redskins 14–7.

But—this is almost unbelievable—our team never made a first down. We gained fifty yards on that touchdown I threw, and besides that we gained only one other yard [on offense] that day. The Redskins, meanwhile, gained more than one hundred yards rushing and more than one hundred passing, but we beat them.

After the game, Steve Owen said to me, "I thought I told you not to throw." Then he fined me fifty bucks for throwing that touchdown pass.

MEL HEIN: The Giants vs. the Bears, 1933

You learned about the pro game pretty quick in those days. It was very rough in the line—a lot of punching and elbowing and forearms and that sort of stuff. You had to stand up for yourself or you would be walked all over. A good example is the little encounter I had with George Musso of the Chicago Bears. He was a rookie in 1933 and played nose guard on defense. George was about 260 pounds and as strong as they come. I was about fifty pounds lighter than him. I was centering to the tailback on the single wing, who was about four yards behind me. Centering that way, I had to keep my head down, looking back at the tailback. Well, the first time George lined up opposite me and I snapped the ball, he popped me one right in the face. We didn't have faceguards in those days, and I said to him after the play that he'd better never do that to me again. Coming from me, about 210 pounds, it didn't make much of an impression on big George. On the next play, he let me have it again. So, on the following play, I was ready. I snapped the ball with one hand this time and at the exact same time delivered one heck of an uppercut with the other hand and got George square in the face. He really felt it, I could tell. He shook it off in a dazed kind of way and then smiled and said something like that was a helluva good shot. He never tried it on me again, and we became good friends. George was not a dirty player, and I never heard of him doing that kind of thing to anybody later. He was just massive and strong. We played against each other for more than ten years and I, for one, can say he surely deserved to be inducted into the [Pro Football] Hall of Fame.

> **"You had to stand up for yourself or you would be walked all over."**
>
> **–MEL HEIN**

Y. A. TITTLE: The Pain of It All

Football is an emotional game, and sometimes you can do amazing things when you're hurt. I remember once I went into a game with two sprained ankles. I could barely walk into the huddle. But once I got under that center I was cured on the spot. In 1953, I played a game with a shattered cheekbone and completed twenty-nine passes. I pulled a hamstring muscle with San Francisco in 1957 and was supposed to be out for three weeks, but John Brodie went bad in the first half the next week against Green Bay, and [coach Red] Hickey asked, "Can you play, Tittle?" What does a ballplayer say in a situation like that? I tried. I got out there and threw a couple of touchdown passes and we won 27–20. You never want to tell a coach you can't do it because there's always someone else on the sideline waiting for a chance, and he might just go out there and do it.

TOM LANDRY: Quarterbacks, 1952

I was a straight defensive player my entire career in pro football, except for one instance—actually two instances. It was in 1952, the year we were getting beaten up pretty bad—physically, that is. Charlie Conerly was our quarterback and Freddie Benners, who had played down at Southern Methodist with Kyle Rote, was our backup. In this one terrible game near the end of the season, against the Pittsburgh Steelers, Conerly had to leave the game because of a shoulder injury. Then Benners got knocked out of the game in the second quarter. The Giants didn't have anybody else, so they sent me in because I was the only one who could legitimately take a snap, having played quarterback for a while at Texas in college. Steve Owen said, "Okay, you're the quarterback." So I just went in. They didn't send in any plays. I was just lucky because we were playing at Pittsburgh and the field there was mostly dirt, so I could draw the plays on the ground with my finger. I'd just draw where I wanted the receivers to go and they'd shrug and go off and try to get there. I finished the rest of the game, but by the time I got in it didn't really matter because we were losing something like 35–0 [the Giants ended up losing 63–7].

I quarterbacked again the next week against the Redskins, and it wasn't quite so bad. We lost 27–17. That game we played at home, and when we got there we couldn't get on the field—we had to scrape the snow off just to get into the Polo Grounds. But that was the extent of my offensive play in the NFL. I was much more comfortable playing defense, as I think you could imagine after my 1952 experiences. Charlie Conerly's job was never in jeopardy.

SHIPWRECK KELLY: Missing (Not) in Action, 1932

Shipwreck got the chance to prove himself early in the 1932 season and proved to be an exciting, elusive runner as well as a fine punter. After six games he quickly became the focus of the fans at the Polo Grounds. But:

For the Portsmouth game, Kelly's picture was on the cover of the program. Only one thing was missing—Kelly himself. When he didn't show up by game time, the band started playing "Has Anybody Here Seen Kelly?" but Shipwreck obviously had better things to do for the afternoon.

"What happened to Kelly?" a writer asked Owen after the game.

"Maybe he's sitting on a flagpole," quipped one of the Giants.

"As far as I'm concerned, he can sit on a tack," said Owen. "He's suspended."

Shipwreck Kelly, one of the Giants more colorful characters both on and off the field, poses with a ball he could run with, catch, and kick with equal talent. His field performances were notably erratic, but his exploits in New York cafe society were legendary. Kelly remained with the Giants for only one season (1932), then went over to Brooklyn with Chris Cagle to own and lead the newly formed Dodgers football team.

The Giants lured soccer-style kicker Pete Gogolak away from the AFL in 1966 to begin a career in New York that would last through the 1974 season. When it ended, Gogolak was—and still is—the Giants' all-time leading scorer, with 646 points (126 FGs, 268 PATs). No Giants kicker has booted more field goals or extra points than Gogolak. Holding here is Tom Blanchard (No. 15).

And colorful John Sims "Shipwreck" Kelly, who never fully explained his mysterious absence, never played another game as a Giant.

Actually, Shipwreck Kelly did explain his absence in an interview that was given a few years before his death in 1986: "I quit because the doctor told me I wasn't in shape for it. I had a small touch of rheumatic fever, and I didn't feel very good—and they weren't paying me very much money anyway."

A DAY TO REMEMBER, 1972

The Giants, their collective eye still on a playoff berth as a wild card, rampaged into Yankee Stadium on November 26, 1972, to play the Philadelphia Eagles. With quarterback Norm Snead, running back Ron Johnson, and receiver Bob Tucker all in top form, it was hardly a contest. On New York's first possession, they scored on a fifteen-yard pass from Snead to Tucker. The next time the Giants had the ball they scored again, this time on a thirty-five-yard run by Johnson.

On the first play of the second quarter, Snead passed to fullback Joe Orduna for a five-yard touchdown. Not much later, Pete Gogolak nailed a twenty-five-yard field goal. Tucker then made his second touchdown reception of the day on a twenty-nine-yard pass from Snead, and Johnson subsequently added yet another touchdown on a one-yard run. At halftime, the score was 38–10, New York.

Later in the game, reserve quarterback Randy Johnson took over for Snead, and a host of other Giants replacements took to the field. For Philadelphia it was just one

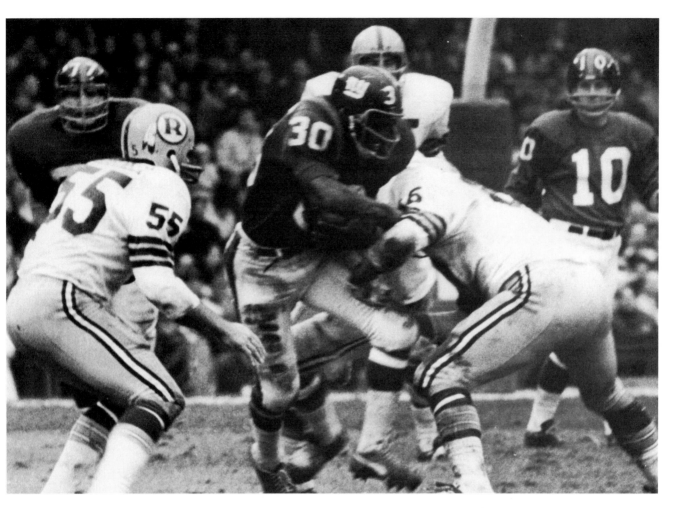

Ron Johnson (No. 30), shown here carrying against the Redskins, was acquired from Cleveland in 1970 and promptly became the first New York Giant to rush for more than 1,000 yards in a season, 1,027. Two years later he broke his own record by gaining 1,182 yards, a Giant mark that stood until Joe Morris rushed for 1,336 yards in 1985. In the background is quarterback Fran Tarkenton (No. 10).

of those days. In the final minutes of the game, [Randy] Johnson hit Don Hermann twice in the end zone with touchdown passes and ran another one in himself.

The final score, 62–10, set team scoring records for the Giants and the Eagles as well. Philadelphia had never before allowed so many points in a single game. Pete Gogolak also set a team game record when he kicked his eighth extra point. Ron Johnson rushed for 123 yards before he was pulled in the third quarter. Tucker caught eight passes for one hundred yards.

A group of disgruntled Philadelphia fans planned to use the game as evidence in their lawsuit against the Eagles. The season-ticket holders went to court demanding their money back because they alleged that the Philadelphia team failed to provide football entertainment at a big-league level.

CHARLIE CONERLY: From the "A" to the "T"

Well, up at New York under old Steve Owen we also played an A-formation for a couple of years until we switched to the T-formation. And that's what saved my life. Hell, I only weighed about 180 pounds back then [on a 6'1" frame]. It was just too tough playing out of the A with all the blocking and running that went along with it.

We did pass a lot, though, after I joined the Giants. That first year [1948], in fact, when we played the Pittsburgh Steelers, I threw so often that day I completed thirty-six passes [out of fifty-three], which was an NFL record at the time; and, hell, we still lost the game [38–28]. So I always felt the record didn't mean much of a damn because we lost the game; you weren't out there to set records, you were out there to win the darn ball game.

ALEX WEBSTER: That Layne

We used to use a lot of pick plays in the '50s and early '60s that are illegal now. Sometimes I'd line up in a wingback position. The tight end would go down and cut out, and I'd cut right underneath him. This worked pretty well for us. We didn't use a lot of trick plays. Some of the other teams did though. I remember one when we were playing the Pittsburgh Steelers in the 1960s. Bobby Layne was their quarterback then. He had Tom Tracy at fullback. And they had to win this particular game against us to get into the playoffs. Layne came up to the line and started to call the signals; then he turned around and said something to Tracy and started to call the signals again. Finally he turned around again to Tracy and shouted, "Goddammit, don't you understand?" and started to walk back toward Tracy. Our defense stood up, and as soon as they did the center snapped the ball to Tracy, and he tore right up the middle and gained something like twenty or twenty-five yards. Only Bobby Layne could get away with something like that.

KYLE ROTE: Gifford's Lip

I remember in one game against the Chicago Cardinals somebody split Frank's lip. It was in the latter part of the second quarter. We were playing at Comiskey Park in Chicago, which was a baseball stadium where the White Sox played. Anyway, to get to the locker room at halftime, we had to go through the dugout and climb these stairs up into this antiquated locker room. When I got there, I saw Frank sitting on the training table and our trainer, Doc Sweeney, who was not averse to having a nip or two in cold weather—and it was cold up in Chicago that day—was mucking around getting ready to stitch up Frank's lip. Finally he got to it and started to stitch the lip, but the problem was he hadn't gotten around to threading the needle. When he realized that, he went off to get some thread and Frank was sitting there with the needle stuck through his lip. Finally the doc got some thread and sewed it up, but I recall Frank wasn't all that happy about the situation.

ANDY ROBUSTELLI: The 1958 Championship Game

We got into another championship game two years later, in 1958. That year we had to beat the Browns back-to-back at the end of the year—the last game of the regular season and the playoff game [both teams ended up with 9–3–0 records]. Both the games were at home, at Yankee Stadium.

The first was just an awful day—snow, wind, frozen field. That's the one which came down to Pat Summerall's field goal in a blizzard. It was a miraculous

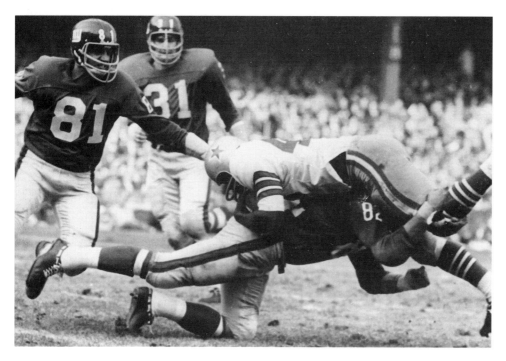

The defense in 1964 may have looked as vicious as ever, but it was not. Shown here is linebacker Tom Scott (No. 82) upending Dallas running back Don Perkins as Andy Robustelli (No. 81), in his last year as a Giants' lineman, and Bill Winter (No. 31) converge on the play. The Cowboys prevailed, 31-21, in a game that was part of an altogether forgettable season.

kick under the conditions. It was a tough game, but then all the games with the Browns were tough. But we won it, 13–10. We were always fired up for the Browns. Then we beat them the next week 10–0, which got us to the championship game against the Colts.

That game, I believe, was a crystallization of what pro football was all about. It brought out a lot of the drama of the game to the public. We were losing 14–3 at the half but came back and took the lead, 17–14. They tied it with a field goal after Unitas led a march down the field. Then, of course, they won it in sudden-death overtime [23–17].

That game was on national television and, from what I heard later, more than ten million homes had the game on their televisions that day. It was blacked out in New York, however, and with the way it turned out maybe that was for the best. There was also a newspaper strike in New York, so New Yorkers couldn't even read about it the next day. But it really turned the country on to pro football. I don't think pro football was nearly as popular in the United States before that game as it was just after it.

BENNY FRIEDMAN: The Great Knute Rockne

From *Pro Football's Rag Days* by Bob Curran:

I think one of the highlights along the charity trail was when we played the Notre Dame alumni [1930] for Mayor Jimmy Walker's unemployment fund in the depths of the Depression . . .

There were a couple of funny things that came out of it. Just before the game [Knute] Rockne walked into our dressing room with a cane—he wasn't well at the time. I was getting my ankles taped . . . I looked up at him—he was one of my idols—and said, "Hi, coach," and he said, "Hello, Benny."

He asked how I was. I said, "Fine."

He said, "That's too bad."

I asked, "What can I do for you?"

He started giving me a story about some of these old men that he had [on his team], and he told me that one of these guys had taken a big step off a Pullman and got a charley horse. He said, "I think we ought to have free substitution."

I said, "Okay, coach, anything else?"

He said, "Yes, I think we ought to cut the quarters down to ten minutes—from fifteen."

I said, "Oh, Lord, we can't do that. There are 45,000 people out there who have paid five bucks apiece to see this game. I'll tell you what we'll do—we'll cut it down to twelve minutes and a half, and if it gets bad we'll cut it down some more in the second half." I then said, "Anything else?"

He said, "Yes, for Pete's sake, take it easy."

The Giants won 22–0, with Friedman scoring two touchdowns and passing for another.

FRANK GIFFORD: The Giants vs. the Redskins, 1959

I remember in a game in 1959 against the Redskins I had my longest run from scrimmage, seventy-some yards [seventy-nine yards]. When you run that far, it's pretty much luck—somebody on the defense makes a pretty big mistake. The play was a forty-eight pitchout, an option—I could either run with the ball or pass it. Actually, on that particular play I got a helluva block from Rosey

Benny Friedman, shown here as a Brooklyn Dodger, came to the Giants in 1929, and during his three seasons with the club was the highest paid player in the NFL ($10,000 per year). His nineteen touchdown passes in 1929—a time when other passers might throw five or six at best in a season—remained the NFL standard until Cecil Isbell of the Packers broke it in the much more pass-oriented season of 1942.

Brown; in fact, I got two blocks from him on that play. One was at the line of scrimmage, and after I cut back a couple of times, he made another great block about twenty yards downfield. Rosey was so big and fast—as fast as a lot of backs. He was really a great one.

DICK LYNCH: Paralyzing Game

Pittsburgh was always a physical game. We won most of the time, but you got the shit kicked out of you coming out of it. I got paralyzed in a game against the Steelers in my last year [1966]—from the neck down for about ten minutes. I got whacked in the back. The first thing I thought about was Roy Campanella, the great Dodgers catcher, and what happened to him from that auto accident. But I said to the doc, as I was lying there—supreme optimism, as we all had stupidly

Tight end Mark Bavaro hauls one in for the Giants in a game against the New Orleans Saints in the championship season of 1986. Bavaro caught seven passes for 110 yards that day. During that year he also set several Giants receiving records for a tight end and was a starter in the Pro Bowl. Bavaro, plagued by knee injuries, left the Giants after the 1990 season.

in those days—"Don't worry, it'll come back. I been here before." Actually, that was the second time I'd been paralyzed in a game. It happened to me in that Oklahoma game where I scored the touchdown and we stopped their win streak. That time I was paralyzed for about two minutes, but it came back and I finished up the game. And I came out of it in Pittsburgh too. I was just lucky, I guess.

PHIL SIMMS: Simms's Day, 1985

Phil Simms had his finest day as a Giant on October 13, 1985, and at the time the second most productive passing game of any quarterback in the history of the National Football League. On that day in Cincinnati he threw for 513 yards against the Bengals. The mark stood second only to the 554 yards Norm Van Brocklin of the Los Angeles Rams picked up against the New York Yankees in 1951. (Simms's mark has since been surpassed by Dan Marino of the Miami Dolphins—521 yards, 1988—and Warren Moon of the Houston Oilers—527 yards, 1990.)

Simms completed forty of sixty-two passes. His number of completions has been exceeded in NFL history only by the forty-two chalked up by Richard Todd of the New York Jets in a 1980 game against the San Francisco 49ers and equalled only by Ken Anderson of the Cincinnati Bengals in 1982 against the San Diego Chargers.

Rookie tight end Mark Bavaro caught twelve of Simms's passes, one more reception than the Giants' record of eleven shared by Frank Gifford, Del Shofner, Doug Kotar, Billy Taylor, and Gary Shirk.

The Giants' offense that day set a team record of thirty-four first downs and an NFL all-time standard of twenty-nine passing first downs.

New York's defense held the Bengals to a paltry 199 yards of total offense in the game, including minus 3 yards of total offense in the second half.

And still the Giants lost that day to the Bengals, 35–30.

"I knew some-thing was wrong, but I kept on playing and finished out the game."
—JIM KATCAVAGE

JIM KATCAVAGE: The Giants vs. the Eagles, 1960

I got through the first four years pretty well. I don't think I missed more than a game or two. In 1960, however, I broke my collarbone. It was in the same game against the Eagles when Gifford got his concussion. Chuck Bednarik just turned him upside down and Frank hit his head on the ground; it was like Bednarik was wielding a sledgehammer. They gave Gifford the last rites in the locker room that day, it was that serious.

Earlier, on the third play of the game, I got my collarbone busted. I knew something was wrong, but I kept on playing and finished out the game. After the game, we all noticed my shoulder was a kind of huge lump. They agreed I better go to the hospital, so they put both Frank and me in the same ambulance and sent us over to St. Elizabeth's Hospital in New York. When we got there, they just whisked Frank away. Everyone was wondering about him, after the last rites and all that.

I knew I wasn't anywhere near that bad. They just sent me off for x-rays and then to wrap it up because it was pretty badly broken. About a year later, one of the doctors told me that when they x-rayed my shoulder, they found that the jagged part of my broken collarbone was right up next to my jugular vein. If I had hit somebody during the game in just the right way, they said, it would probably have jammed into it, and that would have been it for me. But, God bless, I got through three and a half quarters afterwards, and I'm still here. In those days they didn't have x-ray machines in the locker room. Today, they would know immediately what the situation was and would have sat my ass down.

The good thing was, both Frank and I made it back—me in 1961 and Frank in 1962.

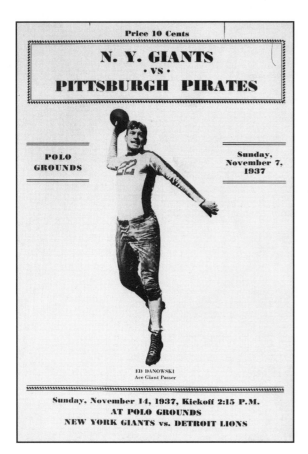

Ed Danowski did not have far to move when he went from Fordham, where he was a standout tailback, to the Polo Grounds and the Giants in 1934. The following year he took over as starting tailback, replacing Harry Newman, and kept the job until he retired after the 1939 season (he came back for the 1941 season before going into the military).

THE OLD DAYS

Was it a rugged game that they played back in the 1930s? Consider this account from the *New York Times* of the 1938 NFL title game between the Giants and the Packers:

What a frenzied battle this was! The tackling was fierce and the blocking positively vicious. In the last drive every scrimmage pile-up saw a Packer tackler stretched on the ground. As for the Giants, they really were hammered to a fare-thee-well.

Johnny Dell Isola was taken to St. Elizabeth's Hospital with a spinal concussion that just missed being a fractured vertebra. Ward Cuff suffered a possible fracture of the sternum. Mel Hein, kicked in the cheekbone at the end of the second quarter, suffered a concussion of the brain that left him temporarily bereft of his memory. He came to in the final quarter and finished the game.

The play for the full sixty vibrant minutes was absolutely ferocious. No such blocking and tackling by two football teams ever had been seen at the Polo Grounds. Tempers were so frayed and tattered that stray punches were tossed around all afternoon. This was the gridiron sport at its primitive best!

The Giants won the game 23–17, with the winning touchdown coming on a pass from Ed Danowski to Hank Soar.

Y. A. TITTLE: The Giants vs. the Redskins, 1962

I suppose one of the best games I remember from the New York days was the one in 1962 against the Redskins. That was the one where I threw the seven touchdown passes, which tied the NFL record [this is still the NFL record]. I wasn't even supposed to start that game. The week before we'd played Detroit, a real tough game; and Detroit, of course, had great defense—players like Joe Schmidt and Alex Karras and Night Train Lane and Yale Lary. The game was a real battle. We won

Y. A. Tittle (No. 14) in a familiar pose. Tittle came to the Giants in 1961 from the San Francisco 49ers. He guided the Giants to three Eastern Conference championships in his four years with New York (1961–64).

17–14 but it was rock 'em sock 'em in the trenches. I hurt my right arm and ended up with a huge contusion.

I couldn't throw the following Tuesday, Wednesday, Thursday, or Friday. I didn't throw a ball that whole week. I limbered up a little on Saturday, but I still couldn't throw very well. On Sunday morning Allie Sherman, our coach, said to me, "Why don't you go out and give it a try? See what you think." So I threw a few look-ins, short passes; it hurt. But I'd found out in my career that you can be hurting pretty bad, but when they blow the whistle you just forget about it. Anyway, that day I told Sherman I thought I could do it. But it didn't look like it when I got out there. The first seven passes I threw were incomplete and I thought I would be out. But he didn't take me out, and when I went back in I completed twelve passes in a row. And there were some long ones too. There was a bomb to Gifford for over sixty yards and a fifty-yarder to Shofner.

I had a shot at an eighth touchdown that day. There were about four minutes left in the game and we had the ball on about the 20-yard line. All the guys wanted me to go for it, but I didn't really want to take any chances throwing the ball. Norm

Snead [Washington's quarterback] had already thrown four touchdown passes that day, and they had Bobby Mitchell, who was always a threat—he was a real speed-burner. Snead could throw him a little hitch and he could be off seventy yards for a touchdown. So I decided to keep the ball on the ground and be sure we won the game. I just didn't think it was right throwing for the record—that's just glory-seeking.

HARRY NEWMAN: Trick Play, 1933

There was a famous play from that championship game of 1933. I got it from watching two of my nieces playing football, believe it or not. It was a little touch game—one of them was the quarterback and the other the center. One centered the ball to the other in a kind of T-formation setup, and then the quarterback just handed the ball back to the center, right back through her legs, and she took off with it.

I thought that might be a helluva play, a trick play we might pull off some day. So I went to Steve Owen, our coach then, and between the two of us we worked it up. We'd line up with just an end next to Mel Hein, our center, on one side; then just before the snap the end would shift into the backfield, which would make Mel eligible as a receiver. Well, we pulled it off against the Bears. After I had handed it back to him, I spun around, faking as if I had the ball, and then pretended to trip. Well, all their linemen were convinced I had the ball, and several of them landed on top of me. One of them, big George Musso, who was about 270 pounds, was the first one to land; as he was getting up, he suddenly got this puzzled look on his face and said, "Where the hell's the ball?"

I just looked at him and said, "Next time you want to see me do some card tricks?" I think Mel got maybe thirty or forty yards on the play.

Well, for all our surprising plays, we still lost. They got a touchdown in the closing minutes and beat us 23–21. But it was one of the greatest games ever played in terms of excitement. I completed twelve passes in that game [for 201 yards], two of them for touchdowns. It was a tough one to lose.

CHARLIE CONERLY: All-Star Game, 1948

My first encounter with the pros was in the College All-Star Game that summer in Chicago. We were up there to play the Chicago Cardinals, that team with Charley Trippi and Pat Harder and Paul Christman. Our coach was Frank Leahy, and he had a horde of his Notre Dame players on the All-Stars—Johnny Lujack,

George Connor, Zig Czarobski. I think there were about eight of them altogether. We had all kinds of great backs on that team: Bobby Layne, the Michigan boys— [Bob] Chappius and [Chalmers "Bump"] Elliot.

Because of Leahy and all his ballplayers from Notre Dame, we knew we weren't going to play a whole helluva lot. So we spent a lot of time up there going to Zig Czarobski's restaurant and bar about every night. That's my biggest memory. Oh—and I did get to punt once in the game. We were really hungry to get to our training camps, and all of us were glad when the game was finally over [the All-Stars lost 28–0].

PAT SUMMERALL: The Giants vs. the Colts, 1958

I finally felt truly accepted by the team and the fans after we beat the Colts midway through the season. It was a crucial game for us. We were a game behind the Browns [the Browns were 5–1–0, the Giants 4–2–0]. And, of course, the Colts were a helluva team who were on the way to winning their conference. It attracted the

End Bob Schnelker (No. 85) is ready to gather in a Charlie Conerly pass here in the 1959 NFL championship game. The Baltimore defenders are Johnny Sample (No. 47) and Andy Nelson (No. 80). Schnelker caught a touchdown pass late in the fourth quarter, but it was too little too late, and Baltimore triumphed, 31–16. Sample intercepted two Conerly passes that day and Nelson another on a less than memorable afternoon.

biggest crowd at that time in Giants history [more than seventy-one thousand] except for the game when Red Grange appeared with the Chicago Bears back in the 1920s. That was at the Polo Grounds—our game was at Yankee Stadium. It was a seesaw affair, and with about two minutes left the score was tied at twenty-one apiece. I got the chance to come on for a field goal. I made it [a twenty-eight-yarder], and we won. It was a very memorable game for me. And to top it off the Browns lost that day, so we ended up in a tie in the conference race at 5–2–0.

HARRY NEWMAN: A Busy Day, 1934

We won our division again in 1934. For me, it was really a rugged year. In one game, I carried the ball thirty-four times, which then was a league record and, as I think about it, pretty stupid for a quarterback. It wasn't because I wanted to. The reason I had to carry it so often was that Ken Strong had a broken toe, Bo Molenda had a bad back, and there seemed to be something wrong with everybody else who ordinarily carried the ball. We were playing Green Bay that day at the Polo Grounds, and we beat them 17–3. At the same time, Strong couldn't kick the ball, so I did all the placekicking that day as well. I also returned punts and kickoffs. It was one of the longest, most bruising days I ever encountered in a football uniform.

One of the reasons it was so bruising was that they had a guard named Iron Mike Michalske, and he was a tough tackler. Before that, Green Bay had the most brutal lineman in the game, Cal Hubbard. He played tackle and was about 6'5" and maybe 250 pounds. He played with the same kind of intensity that Dick Butkus did later. We used to say of Cal that even if he missed you he still hurt you. When he tackled you, you remembered it. I do to this day.

The next week, in a game against the Chicago Bears, I suffered two broken bones in my back; that did me in for the season. Ed Danowski, a rookie out of Fordham, replaced me at tailback. The team went on to win the NFL championship that year. They beat the Bears in that game where they wore tennis shoes because the field was frozen. I was there but I wasn't in uniform.

DICK LYNCH: The Giants vs. the Cardinals, 1961

We played the Cardinals in 1961 down in St. Louis. I picked off three passes in that game. That was the same team that had Sonny Randle, who was obviously gearing up for the next year. A few weeks later, I did the same thing against the Philadelphia Eagles—grabbed three of Sonny Jurgensen's passes. We won both of

In a scene almost statuesque, defensive backs Dick Lynch (No. 22) and Dick Pesonen (No. 25) break up a Sonny Jurgensen pass intended for Joe Hernandez in this 1964 game against the Washington Redskins. Lynch, a product of Notre Dame, ranks as one of the finest defensive backs in Giants' history and has the distinction of scoring the most touchdowns on pass interceptions in a season (three) and the most in Giants' history (four, a record he shares with Emlen Tunnell). Three times he was credited with three interceptions in a game.

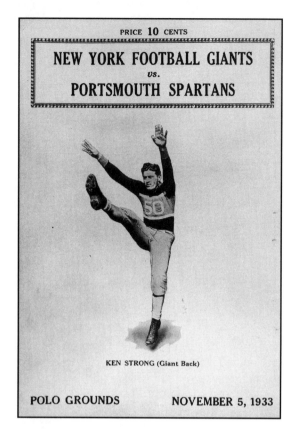

Ken Strong was a true triple-threat back for the Giants in the 1930s. Run, pass, kick—he could do everything on the football field. Strong also came back from military service in World War II to kick for the Giants, and was enshrined in the Pro Football Hall of Fame in 1967.

those games. But I would like to point out—because I think it is very important—we won because we were playing as a team. When I was picking off a pass, it was because guys like Robustelli, Katcavage, Grier, Mod [Modzelewski] were all over the passer. Hell, that's what we were—a team. They thought it was great I picked off a pass; I thought it was great they set the damn thing up by getting all over the quarterback.

KEN STRONG Remembers RAY FLAHERTY

The great triple-threat back of the 1930s, Ken Strong, always liked to tell this story of a personal encounter with the Giants before he joined the team. At the time, he was the star attraction of the NFL franchise known as the Staten Island Stapletons, who played a borough away from the Giants.

During those years [1929–32] I developed a rivalry with [end] Ray Flaherty, the Giants' captain. One day when we were playing at Thompson Field over on Staten Island, I went around his end and he grabbed me in a headlock.

Right near one side of the field we had a small wire fence that was right against the sideline. Now Flaherty started to force me toward the wire fence. And something was getting him real mad. When the whistle blew, he looked up and saw this little old lady leaning over the fence waving an umbrella. She'd been hitting him on the head while he was pulling me toward the sideline, and he thought that I had been reaching up and punching him on the head.

ARNIE WEINMEISTER: The Giants vs. the Browns, 1950

All of our games with the Cleveland Browns were memorable. Almost all were decided by a touchdown or less. We were able to defeat them when they were mopping up everybody else. The closest I ever got to a championship game with the Giants was the time in 1950 when we met the Browns in a playoff game. We had both ended the regular season with 10–2–0 records. We had beaten the

Browns in Cleveland 6–0 in the second game of the year; then later they took us at the Polo Grounds 17–13.

The playoff game was at Municipal Stadium in Cleveland. It was only about ten degrees above zero that day and there was a raw wind coming off Lake Erie and, on top of that, the ground was frozen.

Lou Groza kicked a field goal for them in the first quarter—a short one, not much more than an extra point. That was the only score until the fourth quarter. We had the ball on Cleveland's 3-yard line thanks to [halfback] Choo Choo Roberts breaking one for us. Then all kinds of crazy things started happening. We were, of course, going for the touchdown which would put us ahead. And we got it: Charlie [Conerly] threw into the end zone and one of our receivers [end Bob McChesney] grabbed it. But we were called for offsides. We couldn't get it in on the next two downs; then on fourth down we went for it and Charlie threw an interception. This time the Browns were penalized. So we got another chance, but now it was from the 9-yard line because we got a penalty [illegal motion] before the ball was snapped. We settled for a field goal, which tied the game.

Otto Graham and Groza saved the game for them in the last minute or two. Graham broke free on a quarterback draw and got it close enough for Groza to kick a field goal [twenty-eight-yarder] and they had the game. [There was a safety in the last seconds when Bill Willis tackled Conerly in the end zone to make the final score 8–3, Browns.]

We should have won because we should have scored a touchdown when we were first and goal on their three. Anyway, that's as near as I ever got to the big game.

DAMON RUNYON Predicts

The first night football game to be played at the Polo Grounds pitted the College All-Stars against the New York Giants in the 1936 preseason, a benefit for the *New York Herald Tribune* Fresh Air Fund. Damon Runyon devoted several of his "Both Barrels" syndicated column to it:

It's our private opinion, and don't let it get around any more than you can help as it might affect the odds, that the College All-Stars will knock the spots off the New York Giants . . .

It is to be held at night on a light-flooded field, which in itself is a tremendous novelty in New York and may be the beginning of regular night football and baseball, too, here.

> "It was only about ten degrees above zero that day and there was a raw wind coming off Lake Erie and, on top of that, the ground was frozen."
> —ARNIE WEINMEISTER

They are presenting against the professionals a team of college stars that will include some of the most famous players in the United States, under the coaching of Bernie Bierman, who is accounted one of the smartest football generals alive.

Neighbor Caswell Adams reports from Evanston, Illinois, where the College All-Stars are training, the presence of fellows like Wayne Millner and Bill Shakespeare of Notre Dame, Phil Flanagan of Holy Cross, Amerino Sarno of Fordham, and Dick Crayne, Sheldon Beise, Riley Smith, and numerous others whose names and exploits threaded the football news last fall.

Jay Berwanger, of Chicago, halfback selection on everybody's All-American team, is there. So is Joe Maniaci, Dick Pfefferle, and Dale Rennebohm . . . We think the collegians are a fair bet to beat the Giants.

The Giants won, 12–2.

CHARLIE CONERLY: The Browns

One thing I'll always remember about my career with the Giants was the way we used to be able to beat Cleveland. In those days almost nobody could beat the Browns. They were just such a great team [joining the NFL in 1950, the Browns won six consecutive conference titles and three NFL championships]. Those were the days when they had Otto Graham at quarterback. They couldn't stop Otto in those years, the early '50s, but we could. Hell, that first year they won the league championship—lost only two games all year, and those were to us. And later, when they had Jimmy Brown, we were about the only team who could shut him down. We just had something special when we took on the Browns, and they knew it.

FRANK GIFFORD: Climax, 1958

The end of the 1958 season was another exciting time—we had to win our last four games of the regular season and then the playoff with the Browns to get to the championship game. Every one of those five games was played on a frozen field. We beat Washington [30–0] and Philadelphia [24–10] at home and then the Lions at Detroit [19–17]. Both of the Cleveland games were at Yankee Stadium—the snowstorm game where Pat [Summerall] kicked the seemingly impossible field goal [13–10], and then the playoff, which was on another bitterly cold day [10–0].

We were really beat up by the time we got to the championship game against the Colts. We had guys who didn't even practice the week before. Charlie Conerly didn't—he was hurting so much he would just come out and walk through the offense we were going to use. I was about in the same kind of shape: both knees were sore and I had a huge swelling on my elbow about the size of a volleyball, which I couldn't get to go down. That game, the sudden-death championship [the Giants lost 23–17], wasn't as memorable as what it took to get there. They were actually a better team than we were—better physically—and they had the advantage of a relatively easy walk to their conference title.

A SOFTER SORT OF GAME

The ambulance that stood in New York's Central Park was not needed, despite the ninety-degree heat, as the stars from the Colts and Giants 1958 championship game played touch football on July 7, 1978, a game that was to be broadcast later in the season by CBS television.

Colts players included Johnny Unitas, Alan Ameche, Gino Marchetti, Lenny Moore, Ray Berry, Jim Parker, Art Donovan, and Steve Myhra. The Giants players hoping for revenge from the 23–17 loss they suffered two decades earlier included Charlie Conerly, Frank Gifford, Kyle Rote, Alex Webster, Rosey Brown, Ray Wietecha, Dick Modzelewski, and Pat Summerall.

Myhra brought a six-pack of beer to the Colts' bench for pregame refreshments, but soon referee Sonny Jurgensen had the players, six to a side, on the field. After just a few plays from scrimmage, Unitas threw a scoring spiral to Lenny Moore in the end zone. Jurgensen declared the score 7–0 without a point-after attempt.

Conerly's first pass was intercepted. "Same old Charlie," cracked Alex Webster.

To round out the scoring in the first half, Unitas hit Raymond Berry on two touchdown bombs.

Frank Gifford took over the quarterbacking chores for Conerly, who was now nearly sixty years old. In the third quarter, the Giants resorted to subterfuge to get on the scoreboard. Kyle Rote hid on the sideline and just before the ball was snapped ran into the end zone, where he pulled in the pass from Gifford. Later Gifford threw another touchdown pass, this time to Webster, and for a time it looked as if the Giants might pull off an upset by tying the game.

But with less than one minute to play in the second thirty-minute half, Unitas intercepted a Gifford pass and ran it back all the way for a touchdown.

And the Colts had won again.

4

Giants They Were

Emlen Tunnell walked into the Giants' offices one day, before the start of the 1948 season, and asked Wellington Mara for a tryout. No African American had ever worn a Giants uniform before Tunnell got his tryout, made the team, became a four-time All-Pro, set a variety of NFL records as a defensive back, and earned his way into the Pro Football Hall of Fame as one of the greatest safeties of all time. His records of 1,282 yards gained on interceptions and 258 punt returns were NFL standards; his seventy-nine career interceptions are exceeded only by the eighty-one registered later by Paul Krause of the Redskins and Vikings. Tunnell ended his eleven-year Giants career after the 1958 season.

ROSEY BROWN: EM and ME

I was still only nineteen when I joined the Giants—I wouldn't be twenty until late in October—and all the others there were a good deal older. I hung around mostly with Em Tunnell, and he was thirty-one years old that year. He really kind of guided me around in the beginning. I was just a kid pretty far away from my home and with very little money in my pocket. He became a very good friend.

We were roommates in New York. We lived in the Henry Hudson Hotel, which was on Fifty-Seventh Street over near Ninth Avenue. Some of the other ballplayers stayed over there too. But it was different on the road.

We had it great, though, Em and I. When we traveled around, we couldn't stay with the white boys. So the Giants would make arrangements for us to stay with a black family. Wellington Mara took care of all that. He would check out the people who we were going to stay with, and they were always fine people and had very nice homes. And we loved it! Hell, we didn't have any curfew like the others had. We could do just about anything we wanted to do and didn't have any coaches to check on us. We could drink beer in our rooms, have people in, party it up. We had the best deal. It made me kind of angry when segregation ended and we had to stay with the white boys. It made our lives more difficult.

Frank Gifford and Charlie Conerly and Alex Webster used to come over sometimes to where we were staying. I remember Frank saying, "Hell, you guys got the best of two worlds."

KYLE ROTE on HARLAND SVARE

Harland Svare, a linebacker who came to us from the Rams, and Don Heinrich, a quarterback who we drafted that year [1954] were both West Coast boys. Well, Jim Lee Howell, who was from Arkansas, had great—what would you call it?—distrust of the guys from California and the West Coast. He used to talk about them always playing with their sleeves rolled up to show off their suntans.

One night he was going around after eleven o'clock. It was really a hot, boiling night too and, of course, there was no air conditioning in the dormitory. Well, Svare and Heinrich, who were rooming together, were lying in their beds buck-ass naked. We had had a scrimmage that day, a hard one, and Svare had hurt his back in it. Well, Svare was moaning and groaning about it so much that Heinrich couldn't get to sleep and finally said, "Damn it, Harlan, get up. I'm gonna pop your back so we can both get some sleep around here."

So they both got up and Heinrich's there close behind Svare with his knee up in Harlan's back and his hands on his shoulders, and here comes Jim Lee Howell with his flashlight. He opens the door, takes one look, and closes it and goes back downstairs. He goes up to where the other coaches were sitting, shaking his head and mumbling, "West Coasters, West Coasters—I don't know what, but we gotta do something about those West Coast boys."

PHIL SIMMS on LAWRENCE TAYLOR

The one word that immediately comes to mind when I think of Lawrence Taylor is *energy*. He brought energy—energy to the team, in games and in practice; it rubbed off on all the other players. The energy made us better, got us more ready, and we played better as a result.

Then, of course, there was his great talent. He made great plays, and that rubbed off, too. Players around him would say to themselves, "Hey, I gotta try harder, otherwise I'll look absolutely horrific out there playing next to Lawrence Taylor." He was always

"LT" as Lawrence Taylor is known in the Giants' world, was a consensus All-American linebacker at North Carolina in 1980 and an unquestioned enshrinee in the Pro Football Hall of Fame in his first year of eligibility, 1999.

One of the Giants' first stars—Ken Strong.

into the game. He played so hard when he was on the field, and when the offense was out there, he was always the one rooting the loudest from the sideline. He'd be coaching everybody on the sideline, yelling at us. Every time we'd score a touchdown, he was the first player I'd see on the field, congratulating everybody.

KEN STRONG: A Favorite of WELLINGTON MARA

One of the greatest of them all was Ken Strong. He was a fabulous all-around player, and he truly deserved to go into the Hall of Fame. Ken Strong had been a great back at New York University in the years when my brother Jack was going to Fordham. That made him a hated rival, of course, but we still thought he was the greatest. We wanted him for the Giants very badly. My father had this employee who was instructed to make every effort to sign Ken Strong. But he failed, and we were very upset when Ken signed with the Staten Island Stapletons, who were a key rival of ours. He then came over and beat us a couple of times.

Strong often played without a helmet. He was a great blocker, great punter, great runner, and could pass with the best of them until he broke his hand. When the Staten Island team disbanded, Strong came to us. My father said, "Well, Ken, you are three years too late. I never understood why you went over there for less money than we offered you.

Ken said, "What do you mean?"

"We offered you $10,000 a year."

"No, you didn't. You offered me $5,000."

Apparently, our employee was going to pocket the $5,000 difference or else he thought he was going to save the club some money and make some points for himself, I don't know which—all I know is that that's how we lost Ken Strong.

DICK LYNCH: ROBUSTELLI, the Leader

Andy Robustelli was really the leader on the field for our defense. I used to have some fun with him. We called him "The Pope." You'd put your arm around a girl, and he'd be over in a minute next to you, saying, "Quit that—get your hand off her." Sometimes I'd kneel in front of him and ask if I could kiss his ring. I'd play some mind games with him too. One time we were having one helluva tussle out there, and he came over to me and said something about you're not covering right, you're not doing this, you're not doing that. I said, "Why don't we just switch positions. I'll play end, you come out here and see what you can do." I'd

> "Sometimes I'd kneel in front of him and ask if I could kiss his ring."
>
> —DICK LYNCH

do it just to get him going. Don't get me wrong—I always thought the world of Andy. He was a great leader and a fine guy, and I'd do anything for him. But we liked to have a little fun too.

SAM HUFF According to JIM KATCAVAGE

Sam Huff was a rookie in 1956. We [the front four of Katcavage, Grier, Modzelewski, and Robustelli] used to tell him that we did all the work for him to set him up so he could make all those tackles and look good to the press and the fans. Without us, they wouldn't even know his name, we told him. We loved to kid him. But Sam was a hell of a ballplayer. He could really diagnose plays, and he was a big factor in why our defense was as good as it was in those days.

The Scrambler. Fran Tarkenton takes off running in a game against the Washington Redskins. The Giants obtained Tarkenton in a trade with the Minnesota Vikings in 1967, which cost them four high 1968 draft choices. Tarkenton remained the quarterback of record through 1971 after which he was traded back to the Vikings in exchange for quarterback Norm Snead and wide receiver Bob Grim.

THE SCRAMBLER

The Giants' new quarterback in 1967, Fran Tarkenton, wrote a series of articles for *Sports Illustrated* when he first moved to New York. In the first piece (published July 17, 1967), he discussed his dislike for the moniker he had acquired while playing for the Vikings—"The Scrambler."

Sure, I scramble. When everything else breaks down, I don't hesitate to roam out of the pocket. These wild sideline-to-sideline scrambles have become my trademark, and people have forgotten the simple truth of the matter, which is that I'm basically a pocket passer.

After we beat the Giants in 1964 there was a lot of stuff in the papers about my scrambling. It seems to me that the name stuck after that. I don't think there was a reporter covering the game who didn't tell about the time I popped out of the pocket, roamed forty yards behind the line of scrimmage, and finally completed a pass downfield for a ten-yard gain. And how many times do you think I scrambled in that ball game?

Once.

After the tag "The Scrambler" had become mine, all mine, the public misconceptions about me seemed to multiply. I'd play a game away from home and I'd scramble maybe two or three times, which is my average, and after the game all the reporters would come in and say, "Why didn't you play your usual style?" and "How come you threw so much from the pocket?" And I would try to say, "I threw from the pocket because that's my style."

"No, it isn't," they would say. "You're a scrambler."

"Okay," I would say, "I'm a scrambler." Anything to get to the shower.

WELLINGTON MARA Recalls RAY FLAHERTY

Ray Flaherty was another of our favorites on the team. He was a tremendous competitor. We had two of the toughest players ever at our two ends in those days—Flaherty and Red Badgro—and at the same time they were two of the nicest guys you'd ever meet. Red Badgro was inducted into the Hall of Fame [1981], and Flaherty has been in for some time [since 1976].

Ray was also an assistant coach for us and later became a fine head coach for the Washington Redskins. I recall one particular incident concerning Flaherty. He hurt his hand in one game—really didn't hurt it badly, but the doctor put a big

> "After the tag 'The Scrambler' had become mine, all mine, the public misconceptions about me seemed to multiply."
> **—FRAN TARKENTON**

bandage on it. Ray held it like it was broken and in a sling, and he was pretending to be in great pain. Everyone was very solicitous toward him. I don't remember who the player was, but it was one of Ray's friends and he was helping Ray over to the bench on the sideline. "Are you all right, Ray?" he asked.

"Yeah, I'm all right," Flaherty said, and then punched his friend in the stomach with his supposedly broken hand.

Y. A. TITTLE: Receivers

Del Shofner was my favorite receiver. He was just so good—he had blazing speed and great hands. Most receivers don't have both, but Del did. He just never dropped the football—if it was there and he could get his hands on it, he caught it. Billy Wilson, the player I went to most often in San Francisco, had great hands too. He was probably the best short-pass receiver I'd ever seen, but he couldn't go deep as effectively as Del because he didn't have the speed.

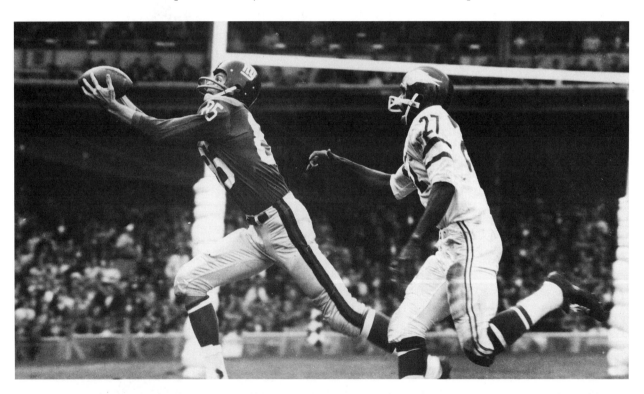

Y. A. Tittle's favorite target, Del Shofner, who played for the Giants from 1961 through 1967, gathers one in during the conference championship season of 1963. The beaten Philadelphia defender is Irv Cross. Shofner set a Giants' record in 1963 when he gained 1,181 yards on pass receptions, and Tittle was the NFL's leading passer that year.

Kyle Rote was also very good. He played the opposite flanker spot for us in New York. He was very shifty and had great moves. He didn't have great speed because he had bad knees. And Frank Gifford—he played flanker in 1962 and 1963. He had come back out of retirement—he stayed out of the 1961 season after he got that concussion in 1960 when he collided with Chuck Bednarik of the Eagles. And Joe Walton was another who I liked to throw to a lot—he was very sure-handed.

WELLINGTON MARA Remembers BENNY FRIEDMAN and HARRY NEWMAN

A Giant I remember well is Benny Friedman. He was really our first big star. Friedman had been with Cleveland and Detroit, but both those teams had folded. [They were the Cleveland Bulldogs and Detroit Wolverines, not to be confused with the Cleveland Browns and Detroit Lions of later vintage.] In fact, my father had bought out the remnants of the Detroit team and brought Benny Friedman in here with Roy Andrews, who was their head coach, Steve Owen's brother Bill, and several other players.

Benny Friedman made a great contribution to pro football in New York, off the field as well as on it. Several times a week he would go around to high school assemblies in the mornings and give tickets away to promote the game. He really did make an enormous contribution. He was also, of course, a fine player and a durable one. I don't think he ever missed a game because of an injury. Benny Friedman truly deserves to be in the Hall of Fame. The problem is that not enough people on the selection committee remember the guys who were the real pioneers of the game. Friedman was one of a kind and never got the proper recognition.

There was also Harry Newman. Harry was sort of a Benny Friedman clone. We didn't have that term in our vocabulary in those days, but Newman, who came from Michigan, was short, stocky, and a very smart quarterback—just like Friedman. He had a couple of very successful years with us. I'll always remember one thing that Harry did in those days. The rule is still in the book. When a member of the punting team touches a punt but doesn't actually down it—just touches it—the receiving team can pick it up and advance it any time before the official blows the whistle. And even if you fumble the ball and lose it, you would still get the ball where the other guy touched it. Harry Newman picked one up like that in Boston and ran it back for a touchdown. I still remember the Boston player coming off the field and saying, "I'll never do that again. Never again!"

> "The problem is that not enough people on the selection committee remember the guys who were the real pioneers of the game."
> —WELLINGTON MARA

TOM LANDRY: Side by Side with EMLEN TUNNELL

Emlen Tunnell was, of course, there around the same time as I was. He came as a walk-on and walked his way into the Hall of Fame. I played side by side with Emlen. I was the left corner and he was the left safety. He was a very talented football player. He never really played the defensive position exactly the way I liked to see it played. I used to kind of look at him when the ball was snapped to see where he was going. Then I had to quick figure out where I was going. He was exceptional at playing the ball—that's why he was such a great interception man in the secondary. He was also such a great return man. Emlen was truly an All-Pro.

DICK MODZELEWSKI Remembers JACK STROUD

One of the truly toughest players I went head-to-head with was on our own team—Jack Stroud. We'd go at it in scrimmages, and he would beat the hell out of me. I remember one time when Jim Lee Howell blew the whistle and yelled, "All right, last play." Well, we'd been going at it for some time, and both of us were really tired. I said to him, "Jack, just fall down and I'll fall on top of you, and we can get the hell out of here."

"Good idea," Stroud said.

So Charlie Conerly drops back to pass and Stroud falls down. I just jumped over him and nailed Conerly for a sack. Howell must have chewed Jack's ass off for ten minutes. Stroud never forgot that, which is probably one of the reasons he came on so strong in our scrimmages.

MEL HEIN on KEN STRONG

Ken Strong was one of the finest players in the early days. Ken graduated from New York University and played first for the Staten Island Stapletons, which we used to call Stapes for short. We always played them on Thanksgiving Day. The Giants would take the ferryboat over to Staten Island. They had a little field over there and people would stand along the sidelines to watch the game. We never did draw too many people—that's why Staten Island eventually had to give up football. Ken Strong was their whole team in those days. He carried the ball 90 percent of the time and handled the passing, the punting, the placekicking, and most of the tackling, as I recall. Then when they broke up, he came to the Giants. In his later years he didn't play as much, but he stayed with the Giants to do all the kicking.

KYLE ROTE: Quarterbacks

I had the good fortune to play with two of the best quarterbacks that ever passed through the NFL—Charlie Conerly and Y. A. Tittle. Conerly was there when I arrived [1951], and he was our starter for ten years; then Tittle took over during my last two years with the Giants [1961–62].

Conerly was quite a guy. He had left college to join the Marines in World War II and fought in a number of battles in the Pacific. He was a laid-back kind of player, almost casual about the game. He showed little excitement on the outside, but there was a lot of it, I know, on the inside. He just never exhibited his emotions. But Charlie had an incredibly good touch when he threw the football, and he was especially effective on the shorter passes.

Tittle, on the other hand, was much more vocal, more outwardly emotional on the field. It was tough for him to come to New York, however. We had had a

All alone, Kyle Rote waits for one of the three hundred passes he caught while a Giant. An All-American halfback from Southern Methodist, Rote was the number one selection in the NFL draft of 1951 and a rookie starter with the Giants in a backfield that also highlighted Charlie Conerly and Eddie Price. Switched to flanker the following year, he became one of the finest receivers and, notably, one of the most popular players in Giants history. According to teammate Alex Webster, "He was so well liked by his fellow ballplayers that about six or eight of them named their kids Kyle."

good amount of success with Conerly quarterbacking—won the world championship in 1956, played in championship games in 1958 and 1959—heck, we had had only one losing season since I got there in 1951. And Charlie was very well liked by all the other players.

But Charlie was old and wearing down. Tittle wasn't any bird of youth by any means, but he was still quite explosive. He could really throw for distance—as good as Norm Van Brocklin, who was one of the all-time greatest throwing long. And this helped when we got Del Shofner because he was a real speedster who could get open deep. Before that we didn't have any real deep threats. I wasn't fast because of my knees. So we had been settling for the shorter passes with Conerly. Now we had another piece of ammunition.

I had one play with Conerly that worked quite well. I would run from the inside slot position and do a Z-in: the right end would take care of the off safety and I would work our wide side, where our left split end would go down and fake like he was cutting in and then cut out. That left the other safety on me, and I would fake in, start out, and then cut back in. I got a good number of my touchdown catches on that particular play. Conerly really had the timing on that one down right.

We used that play when Tittle took over too. We also used about a fourteen-yard hook play with a lot of success with Y. A. He would fire that ball in there like a cannon shot, and a receiver really loved that because the longer that ball is in the air the more time the defensive back has to size you up and cut you in two. It's where Tittle's strong arm came in very handy.

Roosevelt "Rosey" Grier, after three years as the cornerstone of the Penn State line, joined the Giants in 1955. One of the most imposing defensive tackles of his time, Grier played seven years with the Giants, missing the 1957 season for military service, before going to Los Angeles to join the Rams' famous "Fearsome Foursome."

ARNIE WEINMEISTER: FRANK GIFFORD and AL DEROGATIS

Two years after I was there, we got Frank Gifford. He was the Giants' first-round draft choice that year [1952]. And he was a great player—Frank could do anything. It always amazed me, his versatility. He could play quarterback, halfback, tailback; he could punt, pass, catch the football, placekick—a great runner. There wasn't any position they put him in that he didn't produce.

Another player who was especially good but, unlike Gifford, never got the acclaim he should have, was Al DeRogatis from Duke, who played the other defensive tackle. He was a tremendous tackle—played above and beyond the call of duty because he had really bad knees during his entire pro career [1949-52]. He was an awesome tackler.

WELLINGTON MARA on MEL HEIN

A Giant deservedly in the Hall of Fame is Mel Hein. I remember very well the first day he came into our camp. But the thing I remember most vividly is when he gave me a black eye. It was in the early '30s, and I was in my early teens. It was one of the first times I had been entrusted to stay overnight at training camp, which was a big thrill for me. I used to get out on the field with players. Mel Hein was centering to our punter, who was booting the ball downfield. There were players in two lines on each side of Hein, running down under the punts. Every once in a while Mel would run one down too. I was retrieving the balls as they were thrown back and putting them down in front of Mel. Well, he decided to run down under one just as I was bending over and putting the ball down. He ran right over me. It took my eye about thirty seconds to close tight.

Receivers According to CHARLIE CONERLY

I was blessed with some great receivers when I came to the Giants. Bill Swiacki was one. He came from the Ivy League—Columbia—made that famous catch to upset Army in '47. He was a rookie with the Giants, same as me, in 1948. He wasn't all that speedy, but he sure could get open. And we had Ray Poole at the other end; and Choo Choo Roberts, coming out of the backfield. They were the ones I most liked to throw to then. Later, of course, Kyle Rote came up, and after him Frank Gifford. You couldn't ask for better than those two.

ROSEY BROWN: Friends

One of the things I think made us successful was that we were a very close team. Everybody cared about everybody else. I had some real good friends. Besides Em Tunnell, there were guys like Jack Stroud, Darrell Dess—he didn't

> "Later, of course, Kyle Rote came up, and after him Frank Gifford. You couldn't ask for better than those two."
> —CHARLIE CONERLY

come until 1959—Andy Robustelli, Dick Lynch, Sam Huff. I hate to name names because I know I'll leave some out. We were just a closely knit team.

In the off-season, we'd all go home and not see each other until the next year's training camp. I went back to Virginia and taught school some years and did all kinds of other things if there wasn't a teaching job open—just whatever kind of job you could find that would keep you busy and let you earn a little extra money. You couldn't really live very well on what they were paying you to play football in those days. I think most everybody had to work in the off-season in the 1950s.

PHIL SIMMS on MARK BAVARO and PHIL MCCONKEY

Mark was probably the most talented guy I ever threw the ball to. He was always there to make the catch at just the right time. We never had a Jerry Rice. But we had a tight end, Mark Bavaro, and we built a passing game around him. You do what you gotta do, and we won.

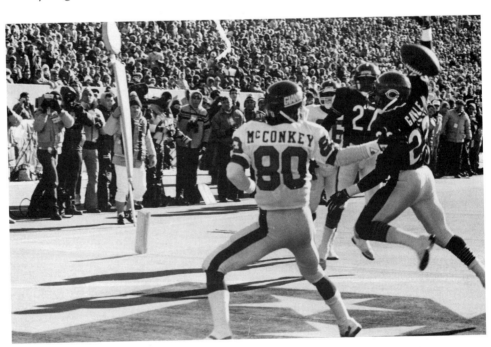

Phil McConkey (No. 80) can't quite get this one, tipped away by Bear defender Shawn Gayle in the 1985 NFC title game at Soldier Field in Chicago, which the Giants lost 21-0. The following year, no one could rouse the fans in Giants Stadium more than the exuberant McConkey, and the fervor he brought out in them was rewarded with the club's first NFL championship since 1956.

Phil [McConkey] also carved his niche in the team. He brought personality; it was an asset in itself. It was just another thing a team needs to have to win. You know, at first I used to laugh at him when he ran out on the field swinging a towel and knocking things down. Then I realized what it was doing for us. I remember standing there in the tunnel before a game and [Bill] Parcells yelling, "Okay, McConkey, go out there and get them fired up." And he would. It gave us an edge, I finally realized. He'd really get the crowd going when he came out. We'd get this huge roar. And, I tell you, it was awesome.

WELLINGTON MARA on LT

When he [Lawrence Taylor] first came to us early in training, I was standing on the sideline watching the workout with Harry Carson and Brian Kelley, our two best linebackers at the time. And Taylor was in the scrimmage. He came flying through on defense, and a big, strong-blocking fullback—I don't remember the player's name—came at him from the blindside and hit him, just flattened him, upended him. And I remember Kelley and Carson laughing, and Kelley hollered out, "Welcome to the NFL, Lawrence."

Something like that had never happened to Taylor before. But he just got up, and on the next play he came in even harder, beat everybody. And the next play was the same. Kelley turned to me, I remember, and said, "Oh, man, we got something here."

He was so tremendously gifted. And dedicated. What typifies him, I think, is that line they picked up with a microphone on the field just before the start of one of our games. He glared at the other players and shouted, "Let's go out there and be like a pack of wild dogs."

And team-spirited. In the strike year [1987], the year after we won the championship [Super Bowl XXI], when we were forced to use temporary players, we lost the first four games. Lawrence couldn't stand it. He called up Bill [Parcells] and said, "Bill, I don't know if one guy can win a game for you, but I'm going to try." So he came back, and played one of the greatest games I ever saw a linebacker play. But we lost anyway.

TOM LANDRY Remembers ARNIE WEINMEISTER

I had such a wealth of defensive talent to work with in those years between 1956 and 1960, the year I left to go to Dallas. As good as they were, I shouldn't forget

Arnie Weinmeister, who played with me before that era. Arnie came to the Giants from the Yankees with me in 1950. He was such a devastating player. When he played for us, he was our left defensive end in the 6–1 defense. He pretty well controlled the entire left side of the defensive line. He was so fast he could outrun almost every player on our team. And he was about 245 pounds, which was big in those days. A natural player—a tremendous player, in fact—but he just couldn't ever get along with the Maras all that well. He was always having arguments about salary. Of course, after football he ended up in the union business on the West Coast and the Giants, I think, gave him a good background in negotiating things like salary contracts.

MEL HEIN Remembers SHIPWRECK KELLY

One of our most colorful players in the early years was Shipwreck Kelly. He came up with us in 1932; he came from Kentucky and had this slow, southern drawl. I remember well the first time I saw Shipwreck. We trained in Magnetic Springs, Ohio, that year. It was a kind of health resort, with big hotels where elderly people went for the spas. Anyway, we were all there and Shipwreck drove up to training camp his first day in this huge Cadillac. I guess his family had a lot of money, and we thought, gee, is this guy crazy, joining the team to play for peanuts, to get his head knocked around when he could travel in such style?

Kelly was not your ordinary ballplayer in those days, like those of us who lived for our little paychecks. He was truly colorful, a man about town. Still, he was a fine football player when he wanted to be. Steve Owen and Shipwreck clashed a few times. For example, Shipwreck would be back to punt—he was a pretty good punter. It would be fourth down and maybe two yards to go, and he wouldn't punt. He'd just take off and run. I'm going to make that first down, he'd say to himself. And Steve would fume on the sideline. Once in a while he didn't make it. Steve would yank him out of the game and they would have a big argument on the sideline. He was an erratic ballplayer but a good one, and he sure could run.

JIM KATCAVAGE: Giants to Remember

With guys like Frank [Gifford] and Charlie Conerly and Y. A. Tittle and Alex Webster and, of course, our defense, we went to a lot of championship games during those years. We only won one, in 1956, my rookie year, then we lost the next five. The last was in 1963, and that was a big disappointment because we all

Detroit Lions halfback Dan Lewis cannot free his leg from the grasp of Giants defensive back Allen Webb in this 1962 game at Yankee Stadium. New York won that afternoon, 17-14. Some of the other Giants are Erich Barnes (No. 49), Andy Robustelli (No. 81), Tom Scott (No. 82), and Jim Patton (No. 20).

"Every running
back knew he
was in the
game—they
could feel it for
days after the
game."

—DICK LYNCH

thought we were a better team than the Bears that year, and we were confident going into the game. After that, we were never the team we had been.

Most of our team was traded away. Rosey Grier had been dealt to the Rams, Sam Huff went to the Redskins, and Mo [Dick Modzelewski] to the Cleveland Browns. The rest were about to retire shortly—guys like Frank Gifford, Andy Robustelli, Y. A. Tittle, Alex Webster, Jack Stroud. The only ones left by 1965 from the teams that won all those conference titles in the late 1950s and early 1960s were, besides me, Jimmy Patton and Dick Lynch from the defense, and Rosey Brown, Del Shofner, and Joe Morrison from the offense.

Two of the three years after our 1963 conference title were disasters [1964, 2–10–2; and 1966, 1–12–1]. Then we got [Fran] Tarkenton in 1967 and, with his passing and great scrambling ability, it looked like things might turn around. He really teamed up well with [wide receiver] Homer Jones, who had been around since 1964. The two had a great year in 1967, when Jones gained more than 1,200 yards [1,209] on passes from Tarkenton and a couple from Earl Morrall [the thirteen touchdown passes Jones caught and the average of twenty-five yards per catch were both NFL highs that year]. Tarkenton and Jones had another good one the following year, which was my last as a player.

A lot of the guys didn't like Tarkenton, but I did. He added a spark we hadn't had since Tittle retired.

DICK LYNCH on SAM HUFF

Sam Huff was a leader in his own way too. He was one tough son of a bitch out there. He'd make a lot of tackles because he would be keying on a hole and, of course, he had that great line in front of him—Katcavage, Grier, Modzelewski, Robustelli; they don't come any better than that. He got a lot of the notoriety. I used to say to him things like, "Hey Sam, is it still the rule that we can't get up until you get on the pile?" Just to give him a hard time, keep his feet on the ground; we didn't want him to get carried away with all the publicity. And he didn't. He just played one tough game out there, and every running back knew he was in the game—they could feel it for days after the game.

I thought we should have won one of those two championship games with the Packers in the 1960s. Not the first one where we got cleaned 37–0 [1961] but the second, the next year. We outgained them that day by about fifty yards. But we had a couple of crucial fumbles; one that Phil King coughed up set up their one and only touchdown. I still think if a couple of things had been different we would have won.

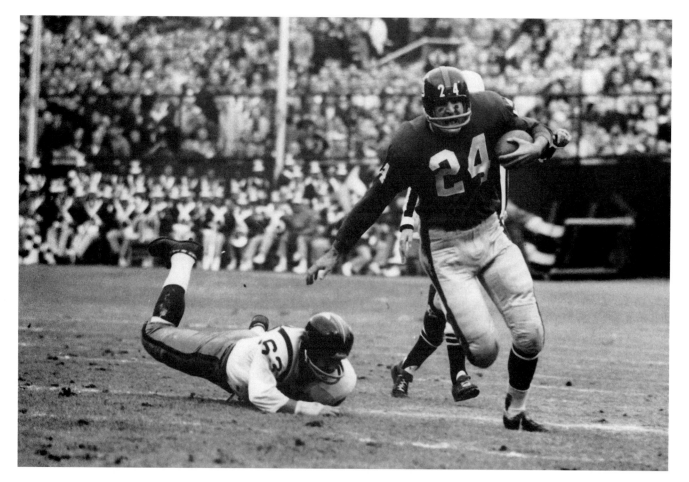

Phil King (No. 24) gains a few yards for the Giants in a 1963 game against the Redskins. A power back, King carried the ball for the Giants from 1958 through 1963. The defender on the ground is linebacker Ron Breedlove. The Giants won that day, 44–14, and went on to meet the Chicago Bears for the NFL title later in the year where they were not as successful.

PAT SUMMERALL: Friends

All the memories of those days with the Giants were good, positive ones. We were such a family—it was like thirty-five brothers. Some of them are gone from this life now: Phil King, who was my roommate; Don Heinrich, who was a very close friend; Jimmy Patton got killed in an automobile accident; Carl Karilivacz and Emlen Tunnell died of heart attacks. It's a loss to all of us who played with them; we all cared so much about each other.

I think when I got there what most impressed me was the intelligence of the players. There was, of course, an enormity of talent, but these guys were extremely intelligent on and off the field. That's why so many of them became major successes after football—guys like Frank Gifford and Andy Robustelli and Sam Huff and Kyle Rote.

KYLE ROTE Recalls CLIFF LIVINGSTON

We had a lot of great characters on those teams. One, Cliff Livingston, a linebacker of ours, was very funny. I remember once out at training camp in Salem, Oregon, it was after eleven, which was our curfew. The coaches would come around to check if we were in our rooms, and then they'd go downstairs to a kind of lounge and have coffee and talk. Well, this particular night Cliff had made arrangements to go out. Someone had loaned him a car, and so after the bed check he was tiptoeing downstairs with his shoes in his hand. He was just about out the front door when Jim Lee Howell, our head coach, saw him and said, "Cliff, where the hell are you going?"

"Coach," he said, "I was out earlier and I lost my wallet somewhere, and I was just going back to the café to see if I could find it."

Howell looked at him and then at the shoes in his hand and said, "What the hell you plannin' to do, Cliff—sneak up on it?"

WELLINGTON MARA: Some Latter-Day Players

Lawrence Taylor and Phil Simms were kind of a breed apart. Besides their enormous talents, they knew the game so well. Phil had a stormy existence with Parcells, a love-hate relationship maybe, but both would come back at the coach if they thought they were right. I think that's what Parcells liked about them so much. It was not because they were being criticized, they took it when they deserved it, but they stood up when they thought they didn't deserve it.

Jim Burt was a character. He was a free agent, not even on the computer. He wasn't big enough, fast enough, strong enough, but we were searching for another defensive lineman and he was available. He came in, and we found what the reports didn't have was that he was a great competitor and proved to be a great addition to the team.

George Martin and Harry Carson were terrific players. Great defensive players. And Phil McConkey, he came from the naval academy. I used to call him Lieutenant, and whenever he had a good game I'd say, "You're up to Lieutenant Commander now." He could really get the fans going, and he was not only a good receiver but also an exceptional special teams player.

Joe Morris was a great running back for us. Too short we thought, maybe not the hottest of prospects, but he was tough and proved to be just the right complement to Simms's passing. One thing I especially remember about him gives you

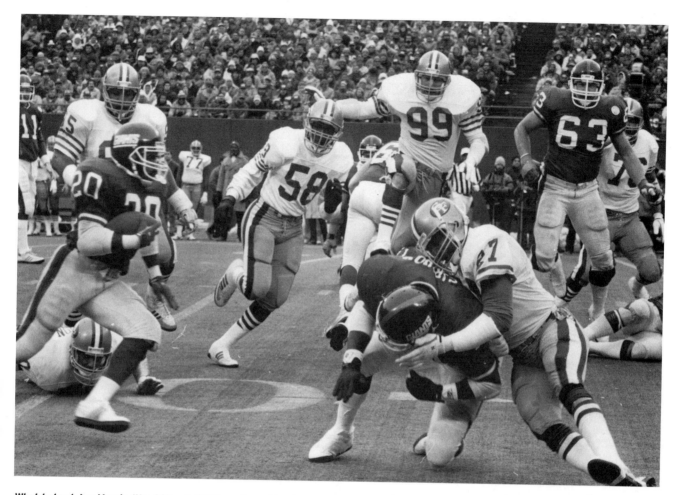

What helped Joe Morris (No. 20) gain 1,516 yards rushing in the regular season, 246 yards in the two playoff games, and another sixty-seven in the Super Bowl were shattering blocks like this one delivered by tandem running back Maurice Carthon. Morris gained 159 yards rushing as the Giants destroyed the 49ers, 49–3, in the NFC divisional playoff game. Other Giants in the picture are Phil Simms (No. 11) and Karl Nelson (No. 63). The luckless recipient of Carthon's block is safety Carlton Williamson.

an idea of the kind of guy he was. It was at mini camp before Joe officially joined the team in 1982. I drove my car into the parking lot that day, and Joe drove in just ahead of me. He had a beat-up car of some kind. When he got out and started walking, he looked and saw he was parked on one of the white lines of a parking space. He went back, got in, and reparked the car so it was just right between the white lines.

Memories
5

SAM HUFF: For the Love of the Game

I got myself up for every game, not just the big ones. It was just a natural competitive spirit—I think we all had it on the Giants' defense. We put those helmets on and we could feel the challenge. Defense is especially a game of mental attitude—desire and determination, that's what makes the difference. When I went out on that football field, it was the greatest feeling. I played the game for me because I loved the game, I loved to practice. I believe it's America's game and nobody plays it like we do. Some coaches even said to me, "You're a sick man." I said, "Why?" They said, "Because you love it to be hot, you love it to be cold, you love lousy conditions, you love it to be miserable, you love misery." But football was never misery to me. It never got too cold to play, it never got too hot. We didn't care about mud or rain or snow. Hell, just strap it on and let's go out there and play—that's the way we felt. We didn't have any heaters on the sideline, oxygen masks, things like that.

WELLINGTON MARA: Going after Grange

In the beginning the football team, to put it mildly, was not a financial success. The first year we were bailed out, however, because Red Grange came to the Polo Grounds. I remember that very well. My father had gone out to the Midwest to try to sign Grange. Back then we didn't have a formal rule that said a player had to be drafted. And Red Grange, playing for Illinois, was the eighth wonder of the world in those days. My father went out to see him—around the time Red was playing his last collegiate game—with the intention of signing him to play for the Giants.

Jack, who was eight years older than I, was very excited, and so was I. We got a telegram from my father saying: "Partially successful. Will arrive on train and explain." We didn't really know what that meant because the day before we'd read in the paper that Red had signed with the Chicago Bears. As far as we were concerned, he was totally unsuccessful. But what he meant was that he had booked an exhibition game in the Polo Grounds with the Bears and Red Grange.

The game sold out—more than seventy thousand paid to see that game—and my father made up what he had lost that year. Actually, it was my father and just two assistants who sold those seventy-odd-thousand tickets out of one small office in the Knickerbocker Building in New York.

The Giants' third-round draft choice in 1956 was line-backer Sam Huff from West Virginia, shown here after intercepting a pass. Huff was twice named All-Pro and four times went to the Pro Bowl as a Giant. After the 1963 season, he was traded to the Redskins. Also pictured is Giants defensive back Jim Patton (No. 20).

One thing my father worried about in regard to that game was the weather. It had been very bad all week and he was concerned about it. But about two in the morning on that Sunday a friend of his called and said, "Tim, look out the window. The stars are out."

ROSEY BROWN: Pro Bowl

I always enjoyed going to the Pro Bowl. I went nine times. The Pro Bowl games were played out in Los Angeles in those days. We never got to go to Hawaii like they do these days. You had a lot of fun at them, getting together with a lot of guys you'd played against during the year. But they didn't pay you very much either. I think the players on the winning team got something like $500 and the losers got $300—in the '50s, anyway.

Dick Pesonen stops Redskins fullback Don Bosseler in a 1962 game at Yankee Stadium. The Giants pummeled Washington that day, 49-34. About to add his bulk to the situation is Rosey Grier (No. 76); in the background is Dick Lynch (No. 22).

When I played in the Pro Bowls it was always East vs. West, the Eastern Conference All-Stars against the Western Conference All-Stars—the American Football League wasn't in it, even in [January] 1966, the last year I went to the game. There were always a lot of Giants invited to those games. Some of the guys seemed to be out there every year—Gifford, Robustelli, Huff, Jimmy Patton. And there were some great ballplayers from other teams who were on our teams, fellas like Jim Brown and Bobby Mitchell, Ernie Stautner and Norm Van Brocklin and Chuck Bednarik. The Packers and the Colts and the Bears used to send the most guys on the other teams, like Hornung and Unitas and Marchetti and Atkins and Ditka. We all had a great time out there.

CHARLIE CONERLY: Coming to N.Y.C.

I always liked New York. When I was a teenager, me and this friend of mine hitch-hiked up there from Mississippi to go to the World's Fair, and I remember going to the Polo Grounds once we got there to see a Giants baseball game. It was really something, I thought.

When I moved up there to play for the Giants we lived on the West Side, around 100th Street and Broadway. Ray Poole was a year ahead of me with the Giants, but he'd played down at Ole Miss with me—an end and a fine one, one of the best—and we roomed together in that apartment there when I first got to New York. We were just a couple of country boys. We would catch a subway to go to practice at the Polo Grounds, which was where we were playing in those days. We always kept saying, "Hey, this is a little different from where we come from!"

When I got there I was a single-wing tailback, which I'd been in college, but down there at Ole Miss it was different that last year. Our coach was Johnny Vaught—it was his first year—and he wanted to throw the football. I would be in a position every time I got the ball to throw it. We made all kinds of records passing because Barney Poole [brother of Ray Poole], who had come back down from Army, was an end—and one of the finest—and we just had a kind of natural thing, me throwing to him.

I also played out of a thing they called the A-formation, which gave me all kinds of options. I would get the ball on each play—unless we had a trick play where the ball was centered directly to the wingback. I could pass, run with it, hand off and go down to catch a pass, all kinds of things. But most of it had been throwing the ball. I had to block a little too, which I wasn't all that fond of.

"We always kept saying, 'Hey, this is a little different from where we come from!'"
—CHARLIE CONERLY

• 109 •

DICK MODZELEWSKI: The Trade

After the 1963 season, the one when we lost to the Bears in the title game, I was traded. So was Sam Huff. Allie Sherman was the coach then. I was living in Cleveland at the time because my brother and I had a restaurant and cocktail lounge there. One day after the season, Sam Huff came over to Cleveland. We were sitting down having dinner and he gets a telephone call. He comes back to the table and I said, "What the hell's wrong? You look kind of funny."

He said, "I've just been traded to the goddamn Washington Redskins."

I couldn't believe it. Sam was an All-Pro. He was only about twenty-eight years old, had a number of good years ahead of him. Then about two weeks later I get the telephone call from Allie Sherman. He tells me I've been traded to Cleveland. I couldn't understand that either. I must admit I was very hurt.

After I told Sam I got the call from Sherman just like him, Sam told all the other Giants to stay out of my restaurant or else they'd probably get traded too.

As it turned out, it was a good thing. The Giants collapsed in 1964 [2–10–2] and the Browns won the whole thing, whipped the Colts 27–0 for the title. On top of that, my family was in Cleveland, my brothers and a sister were there, we had the business.

KYLE ROTE and His Knees

They had me starting in training camp, and everything looked great. But we were going through these three-hour practice sessions with contact, and one day my left knee just went out. I made a cut upfield and I felt it go. I tried to get back into the game four or five weeks later, after we were into the season, but this was before arthroscopy. I played a couple of games and it went out again; so I waited out a few games and then came back, and it went out again. Finally, when the season was over, I had an operation on it.

In 1952 I was playing, but I was still hobbling around there in the backfield. I was second in rushing to Eddie Price that year, but I was hurting most of the season.

Then in 1953, in an exhibition game we played at Hershey, Pennsylvania, I made the mistake of standing there admiring one of the kicks I'd made, and one of the Steelers' linemen came and hit me—and there went the right knee. For the balance of 1953, I was gimping around again, but I played pretty much. I was our leading receiver, but we didn't have a very good year. We had some really fine ballplayers, though—Arnie Weinmeister, Emlen Tunnell, Charlie Conerly, Frank Gifford, Rosey Brown, Tom Landry, Jack Stroud, Ray Wietecha—but we won only three of our twelve games, and after that Steve Owen was gone.

FRANK GIFFORD: The First Year

I had been to New York my senior year, so the city wasn't totally new to me. We had played Army at Yankee Stadium that year—in fact, that was the seventh win of our streak. It was snowing and sleeting, a really dismal day, and Army wasn't much, nothing like the old Blanchard and Davis days, and they were involved in a recruiting scandal around that time, too. We beat them 28–6. I had a good day—I think I scored two or three touchdowns, and I believe that helped bring me to the attention of the Maras.

When I came to the Giants, it was like being back at USC again—they really didn't seem to know what to do with me once

Kyle Rote—showing no evidence of his many knee injuries.

they had me. Kyle Rote was there at halfback but he had a bad knee, and they kind of penciled me in behind him. Tom Landry was playing but he was also, for all practical purposes, coaching the defense, and he made it known he wanted me in the defensive secondary. So I wound up my first year as a defensive back and a backup to Rote on offense.

In 1953 I started out as a defensive back and then Kyle got hurt again. So the last five games of the season I ended up playing both ways. I never came out of one of those games. And I made the Pro Bowl as a defensive back.

At that point, I'd about had it. I didn't know where I was going to play the next year. I wasn't making much money, and '53 had been a miserable season for us. We were 3–9–0 that year, and Steve Owen was sacked as head coach.

The first-round draft pick of 1952 for the Giants was a providential one: halfback Frank Gifford from Southern Cal. He starred for the Giants for twelve years (missing 1961 because of a concussion suffered in the last game of the 1960 season), earning All-Pro honors four times and making eight trips to the Pro Bowl. The Giff is the second leading all-time scorer for the Giants (484 points: seventy-eight TDs, two FGs, ten PATs), the second-leading pass receiver (with 367 catches), and the fifth-leading rusher (with 3, 609 yards). He was inducted into the Pro Football Hall of Fame in 1977.

ANDY ROBUSTELLI in L.A.

As for pro football in those days, you might get a letter from the teams that were interested in you and a questionnaire to fill out. And that was about the only contact you ever made with a pro team, especially if you were from a small college.

The Los Angeles Rams were the farthest thing from my mind at that time. I thought I might be drafted by the Giants, who were the closest team, but they didn't show much interest. The Pittsburgh Steelers seemed the most interested in me.

But when it got down to the nineteenth draft choice in 1951—in those years they had thirty picks, unlike the twelve of today—the Rams took me. They told me later that that far down in the draft they were merely looking for special features in a player. Well, I had blocked a lot of punts and, as they told me, they felt anyone who could block punts well was worth taking a look at. Basically I was drafted on that alone.

So I had the choice of the Giants' minor league team, a couple of high school teaching job offers, and a tryout with the Rams. I decided to go to California and try to make the team. After all, I was twenty-five years old that year and I felt I had to get something going, something that would lead somewhere. Pro football was a make-it-or-break-it situation. In the minor leagues you could flounder around for years and never get to the major leagues. As far as teaching was concerned, that was something I figured I could always go to later. When I made the team in Los Angeles, that made the decision for me.

I signed with the Rams—no signing bonus, just a plane ticket to get out there. My first-year salary was $4,250, about $350 a [regular season] game.

Y. A. TITTLE in New York

When I came to New York, I thought their offense was not as good as the one I had just left. After all, we had had Hugh McElhenny and Joe Perry in the backfield out in San Francisco. But great defensive teams are the ones that win. And that's what the Giants had. There were a lot of Hall of Famers on that team. They had great pride, and deservedly so. And there's something about New York and Yankee Stadium itself. Bill Johnson [49ers center] used to say, "Every time I'm introduced in Yankee Stadium I feel I'm already seven points behind." It was just that you were playing in this awesome structure—The House That Ruth Built and where winners like Gehrig and DiMaggio had played and where Joe Louis had fought.

Joe Walton grabs a pass from Y. A. Tittle in this 1963 contest with the Cowboys. Six of Walton's twenty-six receptions that year were for touchdowns. Looking on futilely is Dallas defensive back Jimmy Ridlon (No. 42).

And the Giants had a tradition of winning. When I got there they hadn't had a losing season since 1953, and they'd been in two NFL championship games in the previous five years [1956 and 1958].

We got to throwing the ball a lot when I joined the team—that's because the Giants had added Shofner and Joe Walton the same year [1961]. We really had a great corps of receivers. And Allie Sherman gave me total freedom in the huddle— I could do anything I wanted to do. He let me make up plays, let me play football the way I loved to play it. If it was third down and four and I wanted to run a hook-and-go, well, I'd just do it. And if it didn't work, Sherman wouldn't say anything. It was a very comforting feeling, the faith he had in me, instead of having a coach on the sideline second-guessing everything you did out there. The players never second-guessed either. We were a well-drilled team and a closely knit one, too.

PAT SUMMERALL: The All-Star Game, 1952

In 1952 I was drafted by the Lions in the fourth round. Detroit did not have a first or second choice that year. In the third round they took Yale Lary from Texas A&M who, of course, went on to the Pro Football Hall of Fame as a safety and punter, and then they took me in the next round.

I played in the College All-Star Game in Chicago before the season. That was a big part of football at that time. There were, in fact, over a hundred thousand people at the game I played in. We had Janowicz and Ollie Matson and Hugh McElhenny and Babe Parilli, but we lost to the Rams [10–7]. The Rams were a wonderful team and had beaten the Cleveland Browns for the NFL title the year before.

Being with the All-Stars, I believe, hurt me to a degree because, as a result, I was behind when I finally got to training camp with the Lions.

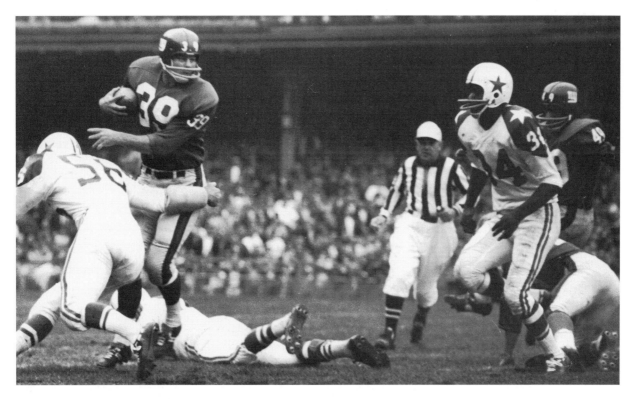

A newcomer to the Giants backfield in 1963, thirty-four-year-old Hugh McElhenny picks up a few yards against the Cowboys. McElhenny came to New York in a trade with the Vikings after an illustrious nine-year career with the 49ers and two years with Minnesota, all of which earned him a berth in the Pro Football Hall of Fame. Trying to tackle him here is Dallas linebacker Harold Hays (No. 56).

I made the team, which I felt was a big accomplishment. The Lions were a very good team in 1952, with players like Bobby Layne, Doak Walker, Leon Hart, Pat Harder, Jack Christiansen. I played through the preseason but then broke my arm and sat out the whole year. [The Lions went on to win the NFL title that year, defeating the Cleveland Browns, 17–7.]

PHIL SIMMS: Super Bowl XXI

I remember going into the locker room at halftime out there in the Rose Bowl, with us losing 10–9. I was thinking, well, hell, everything we're trying to do is working. How come we're not ahead? Still, I wasn't concerned, being down didn't seem something significant. It was just a matter of making a few plays click, I thought, and we'll score every time we get the ball. And it happened. In the second half we made a couple of big plays and scored, got on top, and then the defense just totally shut down the Broncos.

Denver actually made it work out well for me. They were determined not to get beat by letting us run the ball, which opened up the passing game to us. We took advantage of that.

ALEX WEBSTER: The Very Beginning

In the first training camp, I learned it was going to be more difficult in the NFL. Lombardi really put you through a workout. I thought I was going to die. I was a lazy player to begin with—I hated to practice. But you had to work if you were going to play for him.

I was moving into a backfield that already had stars like Frank Gifford and Kyle Rote and Eddie Price. I knew it wasn't going to be easy. I was playing behind Rote at right halfback. The way it would work when I was in was like this: when we went into a left formation, I was the half back, Mel Triplett—a rookie that year—was the fullback, and Frank Gifford would be out in the flank as a wide receiver. When we lined up in a right formation, Gifford would be the halfback and I would be the flanker back. As I said, I was lazy, and it was especially noticeable when I was out in the flanker position. I understand they were just about to let me go. But just before the first preseason game against the 49ers, Kyle slipped and turned his bad knee and couldn't play. So they had to play me and, as it turned out, I did pretty well—scored a couple of touchdowns, caught a few passes. Lombardi and Jim Lee Howell decided then they were going to keep me. That's when Lombardi really started to work me, yelling and screaming at me in practice. He knew I could do it, but he had to make me shed the laziness—which he did. And that was really a turning point in my pro football career.

I got off to a good start in the regular season and was playing a lot. One game really helped my position with the team. It was against the Chicago Cardinals, the second game of the season. I gained 139 yards rushing that day—as it turned out that was the most I ever gained in the ten years I ran the ball for the Giants. We ended up losing the game that day, which was a big disappointment, but we all had the feeling I could run the ball for the Giants, and I think that was a milestone in my career.

SAM HUFF: Rookie Year

When I came to the Giants, my good friend Don Chandler, who I played with in the College All-Star game, came too. He was a great punter, and we were roommates until they traded me to Washington eight years

Looking more like a juggling act, Giant regulars of 1960 Kyle Rote (right) and Frank Gifford play a little two-football catch with back-up quarterback George Shaw at Yankee Stadium. Shaw had to fill in that year for Charlie Conerly, who missed much of the season due to injury.

later. They traded him to Green Bay the year after they traded me. I remember he was so upset that they traded me, he made it clear they had to trade him too.

All of us on defense were close. We got along, went around together, all of us: Robustelli, Grier, Modzelewski, Katcavage. It's like a platoon in the army—you live together, fight together, depend on each other. That's what it's all about.

That was a great year, that first one [1956]. I'd always been with a winning organization—high school, West Virginia University. We beat Penn State three years in a row; no college ever did that before. And so I was just used to it. I felt that that's the way things were supposed to be, so it didn't really surprise me when we just kept winning that year. As it turned out, though, that was the only championship team I ever played on. In my eight years with the Giants, we played in six NFL championship games, but we only won that one in '56.

"We had
Gifford, who
could do
just about
everything
out there—
run, catch the
ball, pass."
—CHARLIE CONERLY

On the Field with **CHARLIE CONERLY**

During the years I quarterbacked the Giants, we never had any real speedsters as receivers. We had Gifford, who could do just about everything out there—run, catch the ball, pass. And we had Kyle Rote, who had a bum knee. He was a great receiver but he couldn't go deep because of his knee. Fact is, the only real speedster came my last year there [1961], Del Shofner, but by that time Y. A. [Tittle] was doing the throwing. But we did just fine throwing short and had a lot of different patterns to suit that style of passing game.

The players would often come into the huddle and tell me they thought they could get open or this or that—Gifford and Webster especially, and Rote too. And a lot of times I'd go with them. There were some other guys who'd come in and say they could get open, but they'd say it all the time, and I usually ignored those guys. The linemen had some good input too. They'd tell me if they thought they could block a player one way, things like that.

They would occasionally send a play in from the sideline, but ordinarily I would call the plays in the huddle in those days. It's not anywhere like that anymore—now they've got computers and coordinators and coaches working things out, and then somebody runs the play in and that's it.

TOM LANDRY: Great Defenders

There was Sam Huff, who came to us in the draft as a tackle—played that both ways at West Virginia in college. He was a little on the small side, and I made him a middle linebacker. Since our defenses were so simple in those days, it was easy to convert him even with his lack of experience in the pros. And he became a great one. After I left he had to go up against Vince's Packers. By that time, however, he was an excellent player who could do so many things on his own. He was also a very, very tough player, a tough competitor.

Rosey Grier was the most likeable guy I had ever seen. He was also a giant of a player, about 6'5", an easy 275 pounds. He had great spirit on and off the field. I remember when we used to have training camp out in Salem, Oregon, and at the end of the day when everyone was really tired he would play the piano for everybody after dinner. He wasn't just big and strong—he had an instinctive football talent.

Jim Katcavage came in 1956 too. Jim was a good, disciplined player, a great team player. He and Dick Modzelewski played the left side of the line—Katcavage at end and Mo at tackle. They really worked together so well.

In 1959 we got Dick Lynch. He'd played at Notre Dame. There was only one Dick Lynch. Very talented. The hardest thing I had to do was get him to concentrate on the receiver and not on the quarterback. As it was, he could cover just about anybody. Once I could get him to discipline himself he could go up against anybody. He could stay right with a Raymond Berry or somebody as fast and elusive as that—if he would just keep his eyes on the receiver and break with him. He was a real gambler as a defensive back and made a lot of great plays.

Coaches

6

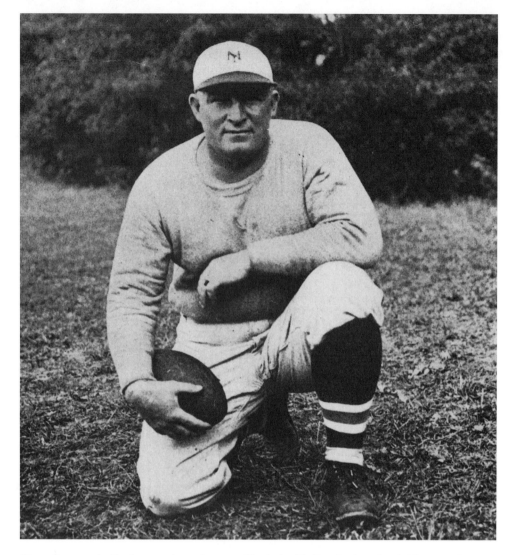

Steve Owen, as both player and coach, was a Giants institution for twenty-eight years. He joined the team as a 5'10", 225-pound tackle in 1926, played through 1933, and served as coach from 1931 through 1953. Known as a brutal tackler when he was a player and famed for his "umbrella defense" as a coach, he was inducted into the Pro Football Hall of Fame in 1966.

STOUT STEVE

Dean of sportswriters Grantland Rice used his poetic pen to describe Steve Owen in the mid-1940s:

"Stout Steve" is the name you've got—the moniker that you've earned—
Stout in body and stout in heart, wherever the tide has turned,
One of the best who has come along in this morbid vale of tears,
A massive fellow who rides the storm in the march of the passing years.

Never a boast and never a brag and never an alibi,
But the breed we label in any sport as a typical foursquare guy,
A mighty hunk of the human mold, blown from the rugged West,
Whatever the odds from the off-side gods—a fellow who gives his best.

PAT SUMMERALL on JIM LEE HOWELL

Coming to the Giants was like going from the bottom of the heap to the top of the heap. I said to myself, here we are again—this is class. That Giants team not only had some incredible players, they also had a couple of pretty fine coaches in Tom Landry and Vince Lombardi.

But don't forget Jim Lee Howell. He was the guy who had the presence of mind to say to Lombardi, "You run the offense," and to say to Landry, "You run the defense." He gave them the authority. But Jim Lee oversaw everything and coordinated the practices. He was the glue that held the entire team together. I've always felt it takes a pretty big man to realize what you have and to delegate the authority the way he did. There are an awful lot of executives out there who can't do that. No one on that team, however, had any doubt who held the ultimate authority, and that was Jim Lee Howell.

TOM LANDRY on VINCE LOMBARDI

It was something to coach with Vince. There was no stronger disciplinarian than Vince Lombardi. He demanded so much from people. He was that way in New York and he'd become even more famous for it when he moved on to Green Bay. I used to call him "Mr. High-Low." I tell you, when his offense did well he was sky high; but boy, when they didn't do well, you couldn't speak to him. None of us could—maybe not for two or three days. He was such a competitor. The best thing that could have happened to him was to get the job at Green Bay. Vince needed to run the whole show, and when he got the opportunity he showed how successful he could be.

WELLINGTON MARA Recalls STEVE OWEN

Steve Owen was a true innovator. In 1937, he developed his version of the two-platoon system. We had a young team and a very deep bench at the time, and Steve used to change ten of the eleven men at the end of the first period and at the end

> "When his offense did well he was sky high; but boy, when they didn't do well, you couldn't speak to him."
> —TOM LANDRY

of the third period. The only one who stayed on the field for the entire game was Mel Hein—he was too good both on offense and defense to take out. One time we were playing the Bears, in 1939, and the first period ended with them having third down and two yards to go on our 2-yard line. Steve changed ten of the eleven players, and they held.

Steve Owen, in fact, came from Kansas. And, of course, we didn't have the far-flung scouting empires that we have today. A lot of Steve's talent-scouting was done through the eyes of people he had played with. They went to football games or coached football teams in Kansas and Oklahoma and Texas, and so we obtained a lot of players from those areas.

Steve Owen was an integral part of the Giants organization, and he was like a second father to me. He came in as a player, and he was one player who did stay

The coaching staff, 1959. From left to right: Johnny Dell Isola, Tom Landry, Ken Kavanaugh, Jim Lee Howell (head coach), Walt Yowarsky, and Allie Sherman.

in New York. He married a New York girl, and he worked in a coal company that my father owned and then later at the race track during the off season. I admired him, was greatly attached to him, and respected him. He kind of brought me up in the football business. Starting in the early 1930s, I went to training camp and always felt like he was taking care of me.

CHARLIE CONERLY Remembers VINCE LOMBARDI

Vince Lombardi came down from Army just after Steve Owen left and Jim Lee Howell had taken over. We all hit it off from the start with Vince—the backfield, that is. We would listen to him and he would listen to us. We'd go over to his house, eat pasta, and talk football with him regularly—me, Gifford, Rote, Webster, and some others.

I remember one time when we were in training camp—this was later on—and Vince came up with this play. We were supposed to work it out of a split T. We ran through it in practice. It was one where I was supposed to fake the hand-off, fake a pass, and then run it myself. We were in an exhibition game and Frank [Gifford] came in from the sideline and said, "Lombardi wants you to run that play where you keep the ball."

Well, I wasn't crazy, so I didn't do it. He sent the play in a couple of other times, but I never did run it. After the game, Lombardi said to Gifford, "How come Charlie won't run that play?"

Gifford said, "Hell, Charlie don't want to run the ball."

We did use one of Vince's trick plays where I ended up running with the ball once in an important game, though. It was in the playoff game against the Browns in 1958. In the first quarter we got down to about the eighteen or nineteen of Cleveland and Vince sent in the play. I handed off to Alex Webster, and he started to sweep around one end but then handed a reverse to Gifford, who went around the other end with me trailing behind him. Well, Frank got about ten yards and was about to be tackled when he wheeled around and lateralled the ball to me. Everybody was on him, and I just took it on in for the touchdown.

Their coach, Paul Brown, said after the game, "The double reverse didn't surprise me. But the lateral to Conerly? What the hell was he doing there?"

Well, I was supposed to be there. The lateral was an option. Vinnie set it up that way. I was just supposed to be there if Gifford needed me. I don't know how long it'd been since I'd scored a touchdown, but it was great for an old guy like me to run it in [Conerly was thirty-five at the time].

On the sidelines, 1963. Head coach Allie Sherman confers with quarterback Y. A. Tittle and backfield coach Kyle Rote. Between the three, they would mold a Giants offense worthy enough to occupy the same field with the team's magnificent defense and help New York capture the NFL East crown that year.

It was the only touchdown we scored that day. Pat Summerall kicked the extra point and then a field goal in the next quarter and we beat the Browns, 10–0. So we won the Eastern Conference and went on to play Baltimore for the championship that year.

Vince was a great coach for us in those days and, of course, he proved it again when he went on to Green Bay.

ARNIE WEINMEISTER on TOM LANDRY

Tom Landry was in our defensive backfield that first year, and he was an outstanding ballplayer. Even then he was kind of a player-coach—he hadn't been named player-coach yet, but he just kind of naturally took over as far as guiding what was then called the umbrella defense. It was just being installed around that time, and Tom was essentially the brains behind that defense. Steve Owen invented it, but Landry really shaped it. It was a 6-1-4 formation—six men on the front line, one linebacker as the stem of the umbrella, and four backs, with the two halfbacks shallow and wide and the two safeties deep and tight.

TOM LANDRY: Getting into Coaching

I got into coaching on a formal basis after Steve Owen was released. His replacement, Jim Lee Howell, took over in 1954. He had been coaching at Wagner College over on Staten Island, and he had also been coming over afternoons to coach our ends.

Jim Lee didn't really want a head-coaching job. They went back and forth a bit, and finally he said he would take the job if they put me on as defensive coach and let him hire another coach for the offense. They agreed. So Jim Lee then got Vince [Lombardi] from Army, and from that point on Vince and I coached side by side, even though I was still playing at the time.

I had complete responsibility for the defense, and that wasn't all that easy because there weren't any other assistants to help. There was Ed Kolman, who handled the offensive line, and Ken Kavanaugh, who was brought in to coach the receivers, but that was about it, as I remember. I'd practice with the defense but at the same time coach them.

In the battle for the 1946 NFL crown, Howie Livingston goes up high in this sequence to intercept a Chicago Bear pass intended for end Ken Kavanaugh, who would later become a Giants' assistant coach. It helped for the moment, but in the end the Giants fell to the Bears, 24–14. No. 15, in the last panel, is Hank Soar of the Giants, who later became a well-known major league baseball umpire.

One must remember that in those days football was a fairly simple game. We had maybe a couple of offensive formations, a couple of defensive changes. That's all we had. So we didn't spend a lot of time like the staffs do today. We would come in and practice in the morning, and then the coaches would meet right after lunch; then most would go home. In 1954, however, I would keep the defense there in the afternoon. I was devising the 4-3 defense at the time, and it was a new concept that needed additional work from the players. That new defense took a lot of time, and so we were always there late after the offense had already gone home. I don't think the players really liked it too much, but that's the way it was.

We got the 4-3 installed and were using it, but we didn't get to be a really good defense until 1956, when we got Robustelli, Huff, Modzelewski, and Katcavage. We'd gotten Rosey Grier the year before. Now we really had the talent and, of course, it showed; we won the NFL championship that year.

As a Giants head coach, Bill Parcells often had a lot to smile about. In his eight years at the helm (1983-90), he compiled an overall record of 85-52-1 and won two NFL championships. His 1986 team posted a record of 14-2 and triumphed over the Denver Broncos 39-20 in Super Bowl XXI; in 1990 his Giants were 13-3, defeating the Buffalo Bills 20-19 in Super Bowl XXV.

WELLINGTON MARA on BILL PARCELLS

Bill Parcells is a street guy from New Jersey who inspires confidence and is just a great coach. Parcells is a great motivator. He's not simply the Xs and Os kind of guy; he leaves that to his staff. But he can lead people. He had people on our team that he called "my guys," and they were the people that he could trust to be leaders. If he wanted to get to other players on the team, he would do it through them.

MEL HEIN Remembers STEVE OWEN

Steve Owen was the Giants' coach when I joined the team in 1931. It was his first full year as head coach. Actually, Steve was player-coach that year, but he only suited up for about three games. He was about thirty-three or thirty-four then. Steve was a very good coach, though, and all the players respected him. He made it harder on some of the rookies. That was just his way, his method. As a result, even the players wouldn't have much to do with the rookies. I didn't agree with that philosophy.

A couple of years later, when I was captain of the Giants, some of the rookies complained to me about the way Steve was treating them—a lot rougher, they said, than the way he handled the veterans. I told them that Steve was basically a very good-hearted, fair fellow, and that the reason maybe he was tougher on the rookies was because he wanted them to know that pro football was a very tough game and that they had to work hard to make the team. After a while, I assured them, they'd get into the spirit of the thing and everything would work itself out. Then I talked to Steve myself. We went back and forth some, but from that time on, I believe, Giants rookies were treated much more fairly and felt more like they were part of the team.

SAM HUFF on TOM LANDRY and VINCE LOMBARDI

Tom Landry was the defensive coordinator when I got there. He was a marvelous man. Tom and Vince Lombardi were both there; they were two of the finest men that I ever met. I learned something from them. I learned what makes coaches great: one word—credibility.

[Dolphins coach Don] Shula has credibility. [Redskins coach Joe] Gibbs has it. Only a handful of coaches have credibility. And those who don't have it are basically a bunch of losers because they lose the respect of their football team. And

> "The reason maybe he was tougher on the rookies was because he wanted them to know that pro football was a very tough game and that they had to work hard to make the team."
>
> —MEL HEIN

Coach of the Year Bill Parcells makes a point from the sideline—and whatever points he made during the 1986 season were certainly effective, as the Giants rolled up a record of 14-2 and took the NFL title. Looking on are Harry Carson (No. 53), Phil Simms (No. 11), and Jeff Rutledge (No. 17).

once you lose the respect of that team you never gain it back. Landry and Lombardi always had the respect of their ballplayers.

PHIL SIMMS on BILL PARCELLS

I had to take a lot of stuff from him [Bill Parcells] every day at practice, and other players did too, with the exception of Taylor. We just got destroyed verbally by him, but Lawrence was so good a player, and had such a different personality, that he could give it back to the coach. And man, we used to love listening to him give Bill a hard time.

There's no question, though, in the history of the NFL, that he's one of the top coaches. His record says it. I've watched it. I see how he works. And I believe in his way. What made Bill Parcells successful was the ability to take us and push us physically much harder than we wanted to go. You know, it's not our nature to go out there and just push ourselves until we're exhausted. And he pushed us physically and mentally. And after he did both those things, you didn't hate him, because that's a skill, a tremendous skill. He didn't make it drudgery, there was a certain spice to it.

Our relationship was good. A lot of back and forth, but it was an honest one. And you have to remember if you prize honesty you have to be ready because sometimes you get what you wish for . . . like when you weren't playing well. And let me tell you, Bill Parcells was honest.

"Vinny was a great teacher, and like great teachers, he aimed his lectures at the bottom players." —WELLINGTON MARA

WELLINGTON MARA: LANDRY and LOMBARDI

I knew Vince from Fordham, where he played and where I'd gone to school. And Tom, I signed as a player back in 1950. It was a great time when they were here; our relationship was excellent. And they got along together very well. They appreciated one another. There was a rivalry, to be sure, but they meshed together very well and had the benefit of having a head coach, Jim Lee Howell, who recognized their abilities.

Vinny was a great teacher, and like great teachers, he aimed his lectures at the bottom players. If it had to be repeated twenty-five times so this one guy would get it, he repeated it twenty-five times. I can't tell you how many pieces of chalk I'd seen him break in the blackboard describing the Lombardi sweep or something.

Tom was just the opposite. Tom knew he was over the head of a lot of players. But he was understanding. I remember a time when Rosey Grier was sprawled out on the floor. Tom used to say to his defensive unit: "Sit up straight, put your feet on the floor, and don't take your eyes off me." But Rosey didn't move. He'd fallen asleep. Tom just went on with what he had to say. The players began poking Rosey. Tom just said quietly, "Don't bother him. He probably wouldn't get it anyway."

Coach ALEX WEBSTER

In 1967 Well Mara asked me to sign on as the backfield coach. So I went in and talked with Allie Sherman; we agreed on things, and I became a member of the coaching staff.

They let Allie go after the last preseason game of the 1969 season—we had lost all our preseason games that year—and they offered his job to me. We were up in Montreal, where we had just played the Steelers. It was a Friday night game. Allie gave the players and the coaching staff Saturday and Saturday night off. I went home after the game that night, and on Saturday morning I got a telephone call to report in to the Giants' front office right away. I didn't know what the hell was going on. I wondered if I was being fired. When I walked in and sat down with Well Mara, he told me he had let Allie go and he wanted me to replace him. The head-coaching job was not something I really wanted—it was something I didn't feel I was prepared for. I'd only spent two years as an assistant—I felt it was like going from a salesperson one day to the president of the company the next. We talked for a while and he offered me a two-year contract at fifty-thousand dollars a year—and I was only making eighteen thousand dollars as an assistant—which cleared away a lot of doubts I was having. So I took the job.

It was a tough five years, though. I'd enjoyed the hell out of coaching as an assistant, but head-coaching was another thing. We didn't have a whole lot of talent around at that time, and I was really a rookie at running a team. We never did really get on track. We did have one good year—1970. We'd gotten Ron Johnson, a fine running back from Cleveland, and he became the first Giant to gain more than 1,000 yards rushing in a season [1,027]. And Fran Tarkenton, who was quarterbacking for us, had a good year too. We ended up 9–5–0 but were still a game behind the Dallas Cowboys in the NFC East. They went on to the Super Bowl that year—beat the 49ers for the NFC title but then lost to the Baltimore Colts in Super Bowl V.

We had another decent year in 1972 when we turned over the quarterbacking to Norm Snead. That was also the year Ron Johnson broke his own rushing record by gaining 1,182 yards. We ended up 8–6–0, but that was only good enough for third place in the NFC East [the Redskins, under George Allen, were 11–3–0 and Tom Landry's Cowboys were 10–4–0].

There were some very good ballplayers on the team I coached there. Besides Ron Johnson, there was—of course—Tarkenton, but he was not the easiest to deal with. He knew a lot about the game himself but you ended up constantly arguing with him. He would often ignore plays sent in for one reason or another, and he'd call plays he thought were better. It did not make for a good relationship. He was never happy. He got to the point where he made it clear he wanted to be traded. In fact, he walked out on us—he was having some differences about money with management—at a preseason game in Houston. We were playing the Oilers, and before the game he came up to me at the end of the warm-ups and said he was sorry but he had to do what he thought was best for his family. Quite frankly, I didn't know what the hell he was talking about because I was working with the punters at the time. By the time I got in the locker room he was gone—walked

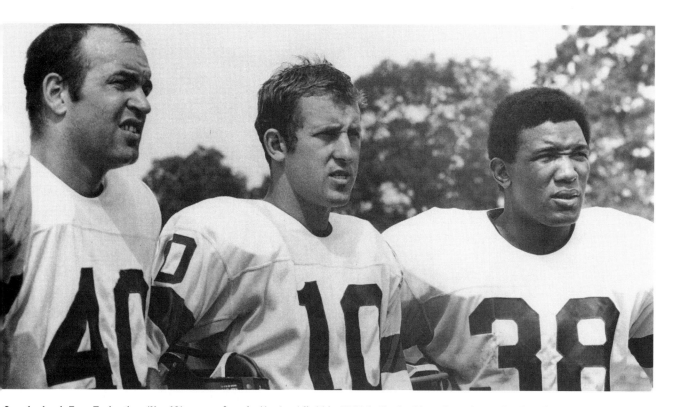

Quarterback Fran Tarkenton (No. 10), a new face in the backfield in 1967, is flanked here by veteran Joe Morrison (No. 40) and newcomer Bill Triplett (No. 38). Acquired from Minnesota, Tarkenton took command on the field and guided the Giants from a 1-12-1 season in 1966 to a 7-7 record and a second-place finish in the NFL East's Century Division in 1967.

out. Well, he came back a few days later, but we gave him his wish and traded him at the end of the season.

There were some others who were really very good. Bob Tucker, a tight end who came to us in 1970, was great. He led the league in receiving in 1971— caught fifty-nine passes. Spider Lockhart was excellent in our defensive backfield. And we had Fred Dryer—he was a helluva defensive end, but he became much more famous later on the television show *Hunter*.

We didn't have the defensive team we had had when I was playing. We could put points on the board, but the opponents seemed to be able to put more on— at least most of the time. We could sure have used a Robustelli or Huff or Tunnell or Modzelewski. I guess I'd been spoiled.

FRANK GIFFORD on VINCE LOMBARDI

When Vince came to the Giants, the first thing he said to me at training camp up in Salem, Oregon, was—he didn't equivocate—"Look, I've looked at a lot of films and I just want you to know, you're my halfback." He intended to build an offense

"Lombardi,
needless to
say, made a
big difference
in my football
life."
—FRANK GIFFORD

around a halfback, the same kind of offense he later refined at Green Bay after converting Paul Hornung to a halfback. He wanted a versatile left halfback—one who could run, catch passes, and occasionally throw them. His left halfback was always the core of his offense.

What worked for me was that I could do all of it pretty well. I wasn't a great runner, I wasn't a great passer, I wasn't a great receiver. But I could do each thing well enough. Once Lombardi finally got that formation installed the way he wanted it, I ended up leading the team in both rushing and receiving for a couple of years [1956 through 1959].

Vince saw the same kind of things in Hornung, who was a strong, powerful runner—and Paul was big. That's why he moved him from quarterback, which Paul had played at Notre Dame—well enough to win the Heisman Trophy—to halfback. Ray Nitschke [Green Bay's Hall of Fame middle linebacker] once said at a roast, "Hornung's just a big Frank Gifford."

Lombardi, needless to say, made a big difference in my football life. He stuck around New York for five years, and those were great years for me.

ARNIE WEINMEISTER Remembers STEVE OWEN

Steve Owen was the coach my entire time with the Giants—he had played tackle for the Giants for six or seven years himself in the late '20s and early '30s before he became their full-time coach. In fact, Steve and I both retired the same year, after the 1953 season.

Steve was a rotund, fun-type individual. He was a very down-to-earth guy, a great defensive coach. His only problem was that he spent all his time on defense and almost no time on offense. So we wound up having the best defense in the league, but we didn't score any points to speak of, and therefore we didn't win as many games as we should have.

Although the Giants were mainly a defensive team—at least that's what was stressed by Owen—I don't want to take anything away from the offense. We had some good offensive players—Charlie Conerly, Eddie Price, Bill Swiacki, Kyle Rote, Frank Gifford—but Steve and the other coaches didn't devote much time at all to the offense.

TOM LANDRY: Owen's Umbrella

I remember the first time we faced Cleveland in 1950. At that time in the NFL almost all defenses were a 5-3 type [five men on the line, three linebackers, three defensive backs]. Steve came in early in the season and said we're going to play a 6-1 defense. Well, all of us looked at each other and wondered what was going on; what kind of defense was a 6-1?

It was the beginning of the umbrella defense Steve had invented—one we would use pretty effectively for a couple of years. We had six men on the line and just one linebacker, who was John Cannady—a big, tough guy who would line up like a middle linebacker today—and four defensive backs in an arc, or umbrella shape, behind him.

"We're going to vary it," Owen said. "On one down, we're going to bunch up and the six linemen are going to rush them. On the next down we're going to send the ends out in the flat, and the next we're going to bring them back against the run or the hook." And that's really all he told us.

Teams had only a few assistant coaches in those days—I think we had three. So that's how I really started coaching. I was playing left defensive halfback, and I thought someone really had to coordinate us back there. I mean, if the end moved out into the flat, I had to know where I was going and where Em Tunnell was going to go, and so on. So I kind of just took it upon myself at practice to direct a lot of things.

I remember when we went into the meeting before the game over in Cleveland, which was our second of the year. Steve got up before the blackboard and started talking about the defense we were going to use and then said, "Here, Tom, show 'em what we want to do." And here I'm a player, and I didn't hardly know what to do, but I got up there and did what I could.

Well, the umbrella worked. We shut out the Browns 6–0 that day, and that was a team that featured Otto Graham and his great receivers Dante Lavelli and Mac Speedie and fullback Marion Motley and halfback Dub Jones and kicker Lou Groza. They would average over thirty points a game that year. It was unheard of to shut out the Browns [the Browns had never been shut out during their four years in the AAFC and, in fact, would not be again until the Eastern Conference playoff game of 1958, when the Giants would once again shut them out, this time 10–0].

We beat them a second time in 1950, this time at the Polo Grounds. In this game, Steve switched the umbrella to a 5–1–5. We had five linemen rushing all the time and Cannady keying on their big fullback, Motley, and five defensive backs out there. Again it confused Paul Brown, because he was so precise in his preparation and he wasn't expecting this. We won 17–13. Those were the only two losses Cleveland suffered that year.

"Teams had only a few assistant coaches in those days— I think we had three. So that's how I really started coaching."

—TOM LANDRY

• 135 •

KYLE ROTE: Switching

In 1954, with Jim Lee Howell as our head coach, they were thinking of switching me to flanker. As a result, I would run pass patterns in practice against Tom Landry, who was an excellent defensive back. Well, before long Howell made Landry a player-coach and put him in charge of the defense. Then he brought in Vince Lombardi, who had been coaching at Army under Red Blaik, to run the offense. Landry lobbied for switching me permanently to flanker. After all, we now had Frank Gifford as a halfback and Eddie Price as a fullback. And then it was guaranteed forever in 1955 that my halfback days were over, because that year we acquired Alex Webster, who would go on to become one of the greatest running backs the Giants ever had. As it turned out, the switch to flanker gave me maybe six or seven more years in the league—ones which, because of my banged-up knees, I'm sure I wouldn't have had if I'd stayed at halfback.

JIM KATCAVAGE on VINCE LOMBARDI and TOM LANDRY

That rookie season, after I made the team and the preseason was over, Lombardi came up and said to me, "Jim, you did a real fine job. I'm glad I looked at you down at Dayton." Then he started to walk away but turned back. "You know, Jim," he said, "now that you're in the NFL you might need some life insurance." He was selling policies on the side in those days, and so I said, what the hell, and bought one from him. I think it was for $10,000.

SAM HUFF on ALLIE SHERMAN

Who did our coach, Allie Sherman, blame [after the loss to the Bears in the 1963 championship game]? The defense. He traded it away the next year. He traded me to the Redskins. He traded Dick Modzelewski to the Steelers. He traded Erich Barnes to the Browns. Rosey Grier was already gone to the Rams on a trade.

Guess what happened then? The Giants were 2–0–2 in 1964 and went in one year from first place in the Eastern Conference to last place. They went to the outhouse in one short jump.

I was very ticked off about the trade. Still am. I make no bones about it. When you do that—trade away your defense, your strong point, and your team comes up winning only two games after it—you deserve to be fired as a coach.

Coach Allie Sherman talks strategy with a fiercely loyal fan, New York Senator Robert Kennedy, who played some football himself during his undergraduate days at Harvard.

Wellington Mara—and I love Wellington Mara—instead gave him a ten-year contract. He said it wasn't Allie's fault. The hell it wasn't.

It just came as a helluva surprise. I was twenty-nine years old. In eight years with the Giants, I'd never missed a game. And the next thing I know I'm on my way to Washington.

But I was able to get even with Allie. 1966—a day of infamy. I predicted the outcome of that game, live, on the radio, over WNEW in New York. Before the game, I said to Kyle Rote, who was broadcasting the Giants' games then, that we would score over sixty points. I said this is a day of reckoning for Allie Sherman, who traded away the best defense the Giants ever had.

I had watched the films of the game two weeks earlier when they played the Los Angeles Rams in L.A. and the Rams scored fifty-five points. It was absolutely the worst defense [the Giants'] I'd seen. The Giants gave up the most points in their history that year [501, an average of almost 36 points a game]. And we had Sonny Jurgensen at quarterback and receivers like Charley Taylor and Bobby Mitchell and Jerry Smith. We had a hell of an offense—a scoring machine—and I just knew we were going to annihilate them.

Well, as it turned out, I was right in what I told Kyle. We did score more than sixty points—we scored seventy-two, the most ever in an NFL regular-season game. That record still stands today.

DICK MODZELEWSKI on TOM LANDRY

Tom Landry took over as full-time defensive coordinator, just after he retired as a player—and, incidentally, he was one fine defensive back when he played. After the first meeting or two we had with Tom Landry we all had the feeling he was going to be one helluva coach. Before Landry, the Giants had been using the old six-man front or the 5-4, and he introduced the 4-3, which was unheard of at the time. But it sure worked for us. The man never got excited, you never heard him swear, but I believe he proved he was one of the greatest coaches ever in the NFL.

ROSEY BROWN Remembers Coaches

Steve Owen was the head coach the first year, and he kind of controlled the whole operation. The line coach was Ed Kolman, and he taught me everything that first year; Steve worked more on the defense than with us. The next year Vince Lombardi came on board to coordinate the offense. He was great.

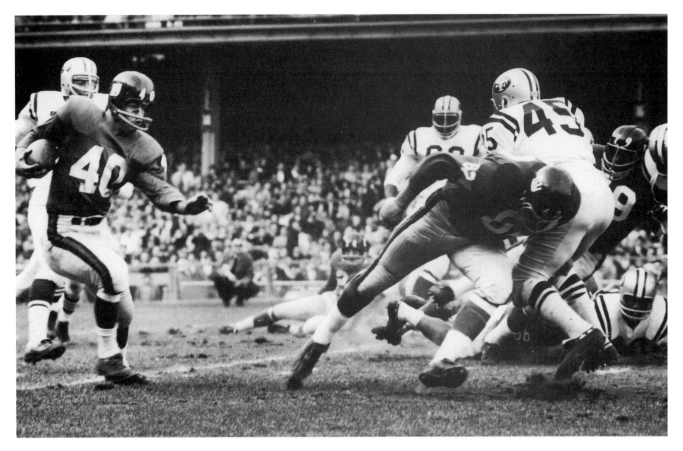

Joe Morrison (No. 40) carries the ball for the Giants against the 49ers in this 1963 game at Yankee Stadium. New York won decisively that day, 48–14, on their way to a division championship. Throwing a devastating block for him is guard Darrell Dess (No. 62).

But you know it's interesting—Ed Kolman and Ken Kavanaugh, who was our end coach and had been quite an end himself with the Chicago Bears, those were the ones who invented the sweep that later was known as the Green Bay sweep. We used it in New York. Vince got the credit for it after he used it so much in Green Bay, but it was Kolman and Kavanaugh who really designed it at the Giants.

After Lombardi got there, they began to have me pull out, which is something tackles did not do. But they had me doing it like the guards. The reason, I guess, is that my forte was speed and quickness and they wanted to take advantage of that. They actually didn't design the pull. I did it on my own because on the sweep I had to cut off the inside man, and I would move out in order to cut him off. But as it often turned out, I was quicker than the inside man—and often he wasn't there, so I just kept on running. A lot of times I was passing the guards, so Lombardi put it in and said, "Okay, Rosey, you pull, and if you can get around the corner, just keep going." I was the first one to do it, and I did it, I guess you could say, by accident. It just worked for me.

TOM LANDRY on STEVE OWEN

Steve Owen was my coach when I signed on with the Giants, and he was a dedicated coach. He'd been there since the 1920s, an old-line coach who had foremost in his mind the motivation of his players—get them fired up and send them roaring out onto the field. Like in the old Rockne speech: "Go out and win this one for the Gipper."

Steve was like most of the coaches in the NFL in those days—besides motivating the players the emphasis was on a sound defense and not a lot of attention was paid to detail. It wasn't a precision type of football, which is what the game was just emerging into. Paul Brown, over at Cleveland in the AAFC, had launched that, and it was to become the wave of our future in the NFL.

KYLE ROTE on VINCE LOMBARDI

Lombardi was instrumental in getting the offense up on game day. He was just so dynamic, so very intense. I remember him at the blackboard. He would talk and at the same time be drawing the zeros and Xs up there and everything was emphasized so strongly—you thought he was going to break the chalk, maybe even knock the chalkboard over.

He was an inspiring man. Players have said a lot of different things about him. The guy in Green Bay, [tackle] Henry Jordan, he said, "Lombardi treats us all the same—like dogs." And Max McGee, their fine end, said, "When Coach Lombardi says sit down, I don't even bother to look for a chair." There is no question that he demanded a lot from his players—he got it in New York, and he got it in Green Bay. But he also had the respect of all his players in both those cities too.

SAM HUFF as Coach

I went back to New York and worked for a textile company. But then the following year Vince Lombardi took over as head coach of the Redskins, and he asked me to come back down there. I really wanted to play for Lombardi, so I signed on in 1969 as a player-coach.

Lombardi turned it around in a year. The Skins were 5–9–0 in Otto's last year [1968], and Lombardi got them up to 7–5–2 the next. But, of course, he died of cancer before the next season.

It was really a difficult thing being both a player and a coach at the same time. On one hand, you have to do everything a coach does, and on the other, you have to do everything a player does. You're kind of caught right in between. I wouldn't recommend it to anybody. I would never do it again. And under Lombardi you had to do every single thing right. He worked you to death in training camp. After a morning session, you wondered how in hell you would get through the afternoon session. He was so different in his football philosophy and his approach to conditioning than Otto Graham. Lombardi was my kind of coach. He made you feel like a team, and you all thought he was God and you were his disciples.

After he died, I coached one more year under Bill Austin in Washington, and then I got out of the game. Actually, Austin got fired and all of us [assistant coaches] got fired along with him. It was okay—I was ready to get out of football, anyway. Edward Bennett Williams, the owner, wanted somebody with a name, so he hired George Allen away from the Rams. Allen came to Washington and brought practically his whole team—especially the defense, which was his specialty. Hell, he even brought his secretary, towel boys, everybody. He had that philosophy: the future is now! It was a good time to look at the rest of my life, put football aside, and see what else was out there in the world.

7
Enemies Remembered

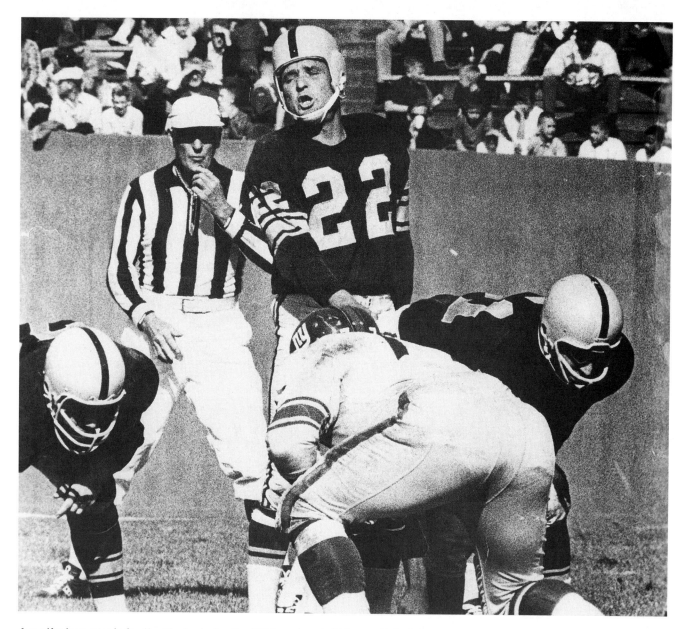

A particular nemesis for the Giants during the 1950s and early '60s was Hall of Fame quarterback Bobby Layne, who led the Lions from 1950 through 1958 and the Steelers, for whom he is calling signals here in a game against the Giants, from 1958 through 1962. Many remembered Layne for his wildness off the field, as well as his great talent on it.

ALEX WEBSTER Remembers BOBBY LAYNE

Layne was great—a true and colorful character. He wouldn't take any guff from anybody, and he was a wild man. I remember when I went to talk to the Lions before I signed with the Giants. It was the last game of the 1954 [NFL] season. They were playing in Cleveland and I went there. I met with their general manager, and after the game I went out to the airport with the team. They were going back to Detroit, and I was going to Newark. Well, I'd never seen anything like it. There was Layne walking through the airport with a case of beer under his arm. With him was Les Bingaman, one of their defensive linemen who weighed about 320 pounds. He said to me, "C'mon with us, kid, and we'll make something out of you. Maybe we won't make you play any better, but we'll sure be able to teach you to drink with us." They were quite a group of characters, and Bobby was their ringleader.

Another story about Bobby was when he was with Pittsburgh—this was somewhere around 1960. They were in town to play us, and their coach, Buddy Parker, cornered Bobby and his roommate, Ernie Stautner, on Saturday. "We really need to win this game tomorrow," he told them, "so I want you two guys to be sure to get in early tonight, to make curfew."

So Bobby said to him, "Don't worry about it." Well, that night they got back at about ten-thirty—eleven o'clock was curfew—and went to their room. They put the television on and Ernie went to bed. About eleven-thirty, Bobby sat down and wrote a note that said something like this:

> Buddy,
> Ernie and I got home at ten-thirty. It's now eleven-thirty and Ernie's asleep and I'm going out of my goddamn mind. Don't worry, I'll play good tomorrow.
>
> Bobby
>
> P.S. Here's my fine money.

He put the note and the money in an envelope and on his way out slipped it under the door to Buddy Parker's room. Word was that he closed P. J. Clarke's at four in the morning. And then he came out and threw three touchdown passes against us that afternoon.

BRONKO NAGURSKI: MEL HEIN's Nemesis

I learned that if you hit Bronko Nagurski by yourself you were in trouble: if you hit him low, he'd trample you to death; if you hit him high, he'd take you about ten yards. The best way to tackle Bronko was to have your teammates hit him about the same time—one or two low, one or two high. He was the most powerful fullback that I ever played against in all my career. He had a big body and

> **"They were quite a group of characters, and Bobby was their ringleader."**
> —ALEX WEBSTER

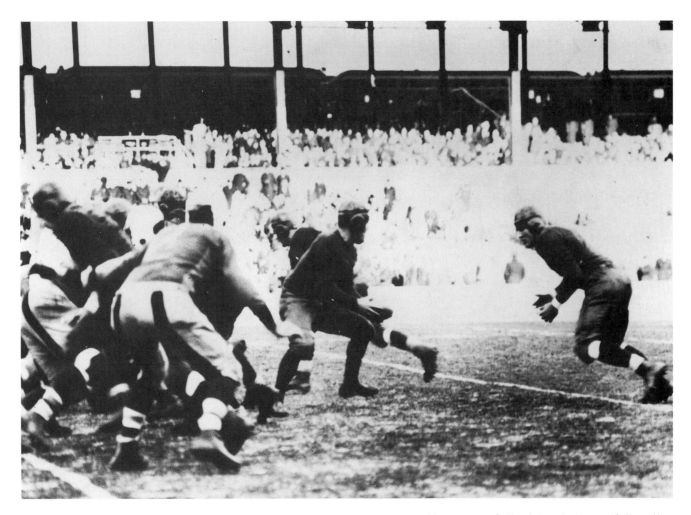

One of the most formidable opponents the Giants ever had to contend with was Chicago Bears fullback Bronko Nagurski. Here the notoriously powerful Nagurski is about to take a pitchout from Bear quarterback Carl Brumbaugh in the 1934 NFL title game against the Giants, which became known as the "Sneakers Championship," after the New Yorkers donned sneakers for the second half and turned a 10-3 deficit into a 30-13 victory.

could get that body, that trunk, down and be able to throw his shoulder into you. If you didn't get under his shoulder, he just knocked you butt over tea kettles.

Another thing about Bronko was his blocking. The Bears had this little scatback in those days by the name of Beattie Feathers. Well, Bronko could open up the whole defensive line for him. He would burst it open, and Feathers would be right on his butt, following him through, and then he'd break one way or the other. It gave Feathers an advantage no other running back had, and he set a rushing record in 1934, over one thousand yards [1,004], the first ever to do that. After that year we worked at special defenses to go up against that, and we were able to stop Feathers pretty well in later years.

PHIL SIMMS and the Steelers

One of the greatest moments with the Giants for me to remember was also my first experience playing in a game in the pros. It was a preseason game in Pittsburgh against the three-time (soon-to-be four-time) Super Bowl–champion Steelers. I was going to get to play against the guys I had watched on television when I was growing up. The Steelers and the Cowboys, they were the best teams of that era. I was a product of those two teams; all through high school and college I really identified with them.

To play on the same field, in the same game, with Terry Bradshaw, I couldn't even comprehend it. To walk up to the line of scrimmage and see staring back at you Mean Joe Greene, Jack Ham, Jack Lambert, Mel Blount. I mean, I was going, "Hell, I want to get some autographs. This team is unbelievable." It was such an incredible experience to be on a field with those people.

"I was going to get to play against the guys I had watched on television when I was growing up."
—PHIL SIMMS

FRANK GIFFORD on CHUCK BEDNARIK

I sat out the 1961 season after I got a concussion near the end of the 1960 season [in a game against the Philadelphia Eagles]. I did quite a bit of radio that year and my local television show. When I came back in 1962, I kept working on television at the same time.

The thing about the concussion comes up all the time—about the hit I took from Chuck Bednarik. Was it a cheap shot? What do I think about it? Well, it's all a lot of bull made up by a lot of people who don't understand what this game is about. I get real tired hearing about it.

I remember Kathie came home one day not long after we were married and said, "Who's Bednarik?" I said, "It's not somebody, it's a pasta." I told her, "You're going to hear that name a whole helluva lot." Nobody seems to be able to forget about the incident. Bednarik has perpetuated it more than anybody. But he's a good guy, and I have no animosity. I was simply looking back to catch a football and he hit me just right and knocked me over. I ended up with a concussion—that's all.

SAM HUFF on JIM TAYLOR

Green Bay had a great team under Lombardi. They also had one guy I loved to hit and that was [fullback] Jim Taylor. He was a ferocious ballplayer. It's interesting how an offensive guy is never considered ferocious, but defensive players are.

Throughout their careers Giant linebacker Sam Huff and Green Bay Packer fullback Jim Taylor (No. 31), carrying the ball here in a 1962 game against the Giants, had a very special feud. Both survived their brutal encounters on the field and made it to the Hall of Fame, Taylor in 1976 and Huff in 1982. Giant defenders here are linebacker Tom Scott (No. 82) and end Andy Robustelli (No. 81). The other Packer is halfback Paul Hornung (No. 5).

Well, that just isn't the case. A guy like Taylor is every bit as competitive and vicious as a defensive player. We really went at it. I remember denting my helmet hitting that sucker.

People often say, "But you were still friends?" When were you friends with Taylor when he was playing against you? Did Taylor have any friends? Did [Bears linebacker Dick] Butkus have any friends? Did [Packers linebacker Ray] Nitschke have any friends? Linebackers don't make friends very easily.

RED BADGRO Remembers JOHNNY BLOOD MCNALLY

I remember a situation that involved Johnny Blood [McNally]. We were playing Green Bay in New York and we were leading 13–7. They were down on our goal line and they ran the ball three times but didn't make it. There were just seconds left, and I sensed they wouldn't run at us on fourth down, the last play of the game for them. They had a play they relied on a lot in those days. It was a quick pass to Johnny Blood out in the flat—a fake to the fullback first and then out to Johnny. It would work in this instance, they thought, because there was only a yard to go and we'd be bunched up to stop Hinkle if he tried to bull it in. I still didn't think they would run it, and so I kept my eye on Blood—and sure enough I saw him take off for the flat. I said, to hell with it, and I just ran across the line of scrimmage and tackled him in the backfield. When the quarterback looked up from his fake to throw the ball, all he saw was Johnny and me on the ground. He was standing there with the ball and no one to throw it to. Then our fellows smothered him. The referee didn't call anything, and we won the game. Things like that you remember.

> "When the quarterback looked up from his fake to throw the ball, all he saw was Johnny and me on the ground."
>
> —RED BADGRO

ARNIE WEINMEISTER Remembers the Redskins

A team we had a strong rivalry with in those days was the Washington Redskins. They didn't have all that good a team in those years—Sammy Baugh was at the end of his career, in his late thirties. But they always gave us trouble, for some reason or another. I guess they really got up for the games against the Giants. They did have some good players, though: [halfback] Bullet Bill Dudley was with them then; Bones Taylor was a terrific end, and Gene Brito was a good one too; and Al DeMao, who played center and linebacker, was a tough one. They beat us at the end of the 1952 season, which knocked us out of the running for the conference title [the Giants ended up a game behind the Browns that year]. And they beat us twice my last year [1953].

JIM KATCAVAGE: Worth Remembering

Our defensive line worked very well right from the start. We had different maneuvers we worked out. One thing was called "the twist" between me and Mo; others involved all four of us. The tricks—or schemes—were all geared to throw off the offensive line of the other team, surprise them. We just worked together very well as a unit.

You had to have different things going for you on the defensive line in those days. There were so many good offensive linemen when I came up in 1956, and they were all bigger than I was and a lot bigger than those guys I'd played against when I was with Dayton. There was Bob St. Clair of the 49ers—he was about 6'9"

"Hubbard
was the left
defensive
tackle, and
he stopped
everything."

—MEL HEIN

and 265 pounds, and he's in the Hall of Fame now. So is Forrest Gregg, who was with the Packers—he was about 6'4" and 240. And Lou Creekmur of the Lions and Mike McCormack of the Browns. The next year Jim Parker came on with the Colts, and there probably has never been a better offensive tackle in the NFL. He was over 260 and fast. Rosey Brown, who played for us, is the only offensive tackle who rates as high as Parker, in my opinion.

CAL HUBBARD According to MEL HEIN

Probably the greatest tackle I ever played against was Cal Hubbard of the Packers. We were playing up at Green Bay one time and the score was 0–0 at the half. Hubbard was the left defensive tackle, and he stopped everything. We used to like to run to our right from the single wing, running to the strong side of the line— that was our normal tactic out of that formation. But against the Packers that meant we would be running into Cal Hubbard's side of the line. So we changed it and were running everything to the left that day. Well, we were making yardage because we were running away from Hubbard. Between halves they decided to move Cal to middle linebacker. They had a seven-man line and set him up right behind them as a solo linebacker. From that position the son of a gun made tackles all over the field and they finally beat us, 6–0.

ANDY ROBUSTELLI: The Toughest I Remember

The Colts were a great football team. They had perhaps the best player I ever went up against, [offensive tackle] Jim Parker. We were playing a defense that was a little different—basically a five-man line, and then we started to get into the four, and sometimes the three. We played a changing defense. And it put people like me and other defensive ends who were relatively light (I was about 235 by then; so was our other defensive end, Jim Katcavage) in a position where Katcavage and I had to go up against interior offensive linemen who were much bigger. Parker, for example, was 6'3" and 270 pounds and still very agile and quick, and I often ended up playing off him. He was outstanding.

SAM HUFF's Ultimate Challenge

I guess what I loved most about the game was tackling. I loved going up against guys like Jimmy Brown and Jim Taylor. I'd look across the line of scrimmage and

I'd see those guys in the backfield, and I knew they were going to get the ball. That was the challenge—I was going to get the chance to hit them. They were great and powerful, and they were the ultimate challenge for me. I loved it.

ARNIE WEINMEISTER: Browns to Remember

There were a lot of great players out there in the early 1950s. Otto Graham, the quarterback of the Browns, was especially effective. The Browns, of course, were the perennial champions in the All-America Conference and also when they went to the National Football League. Lou Rymkus, an offensive tackle for Cleveland, is another I always considered outstanding—I used to go toe-to-toe with him. And [fullback] Marion Motley was really a horse. They used to have a trap play—called a 32-trap, I believe—where he ran up the middle. One game, Otto Schnellbacher, an All-Pro safety we had then—he was also a professional basketball player at the time for Providence—met Motley head-on, and Motley never even broke stride going for the goal line. Schnellbacher was knocked over backwards by Motley and knocked out cold. From that day forward, Schnellbacher said, "When that guy comes through, all I'm going to do is wait till he goes by and grab onto the back of his shoulder pads and take a ride. I'm never going to meet him head-on again."

DICK MODZELEWSKI on ERNIE STAUTNER

Talk about tough: a guy I teamed with on the Steelers, Ernie Stautner, set the standard. I never had to play against him, fortunately, because he was a defensive tackle too. I remember one time we played the Pittsburgh Steelers, and after the game Jim Lee Howell said, "I want to congratulate Rosey Brown and Darrell Dess, who did a great job of containing Ernie Stautner today." They both rolled their eyes; the next day both of them were in the treatment room. They couldn't practice for the next two days because Ernie had just beat the living hell out of them.

RED BADGRO on CLARKE HINKLE

We had some good games against the Packers in those years. I remember a couple of incidents. One involved Clarke Hinkle, their fullback, a great runner. Well, we were playing at Green Bay and leading 10–7. It was late in the game, and we had kicked off to them. Hinkle got the ball, broke out to the

> "I guess what I loved most about the game was tackling."
> —SAM HUFF

side with it, and had a blocker in front of him. I don't know where the rest of our team was, but suddenly there was only me between him and his blocker and the end zone. I figured I had to get him some way or they would win the ball game. The odds sure weren't with me because Hinkle was such a powerful runner. He didn't even need that blocker, probably. And he had the goal line in his eyes. I don't know exactly how it happened, but I held off the blocker and Hinkle ran right into him, bounced off, and hurtled into my arms. We both went down and the blocker ended up on top of us. I know Clarke would love to have that play over, because probably ninety-nine times out of a hundred he would have scored. He was more surprised than I was when he found himself on the ground. Afterward he told me he thought his blocker had tackled him.

DICK MODZELEWSKI: Some of the Very Best

The best backfield I think I ever went up against was the 49ers in the 1950s. Hugh McElhenny was a great runner, one of the hardest to nail who ever played the game. And they had that great fullback, Joe Perry, and Y. A. Tittle at quarterback. The one play they used so well was Tittle dropping back and dumping a screen pass to McElhenny. It was very effective. Tittle used the same kind of pass a lot when he came to the Giants in the 1960s.

The best running back—no question—Jim Brown of Cleveland. One time they showed film after a game with the Browns, and here was Jimmy Brown going up the middle and there are about six or seven of us on him, underneath him, everywhere, and we could not bring the son of a bitch down for about ten yards. The only way to stop Brown was to gang-tackle him.

DICK LYNCH: Backs to Remember

There's a lot to remember from those days. There were some backs that were really tough to tackle—guys like Jimmy Brown, John David Crow, Jim Taylor. There were some receivers really tough to cover. I remember one day I held Sonny Randle of the Cardinals to sixteen catches—that was in 1962. I think it was close to an NFL record [at the time only Tom Fears of the Rams had ever caught more passes in a game—eighteen]. He didn't catch all sixteen off me, but it was a rough day—what I like to call an astigmatism day.

ARNIE WEINMEISTER: Eagles of Note

Philadelphia was a good team. They, of course, had Steve Van Buren, probably one of the best running backs I ever saw. He was big, strong, fast—great moves. He was also at the end of his career when I played against him. And they had Tommy Thompson at quarterback and Pete Pihos at end. Then there was Chuck Bednarik, I think probably the greatest of all the sixty-minute players, at center and linebacker. And Al Wistert and Bucko Kilroy played on their offensive line—they didn't come any better than those two. They were not the team they'd been in the late 1940s when they won the NFL title [twice, in 1948 and 1949, and they lost it to the Cardinals in the 1947 championship game]. But they beat us in '52 too, like the Redskins, which helped keep us behind the Browns.

> "It was a rough day-
> what I like
> to call an
> astigmatism
> day."
>
> —DICK LYNCH

The mighty front four of the Giants—Dick Modzelewski (No. 77), Andy Robustelli (No. 81), Rosey Grier (No. 76), and Jim Katcavage—do battle while Jim Brown waits in the flat for a pass from Frank Ryan (No. 13) in this game against the Cleveland Browns. The Giants and the Browns waged war quite a few times for the NFL East crown in the 1950s and early 1960s.

"In those days
we didn't wear
face masks-
but I guess a
face mask
wouldn't
have helped
anyway."
-ROSEY BROWN

ROSEY BROWN: Tough Ones

A good one was Len Ford of the Browns—he was so big and quick, a great athlete; he had the whole package. Ernie Stautner of Pittsburgh was also a brutal one—he just kept coming after you, and he never quit, never slowed down, just kept coming. We really had some battles, Stautner and I, because he never would give up. We might be twenty, twenty-five points ahead, but it didn't matter, didn't change things one bit as far as Ernie was concerned.

They all had their tactics, some of them pretty strange. I remember this guy Don Cob, who played defensive tackle for the Cleveland Browns. He liked to chew tobacco. He was a big guy too, maybe 260 pounds, about 6'3". The first time I went up against him in 1953 he spit tobacco at me. And in those days we didn't wear face masks—but I guess a face mask wouldn't have helped anyway. He did it later too. You'd get down and get in your stance and he'd spit his tobacco across the line of scrimmage at you. He did it, I guess, to throw your rhythm off. I finally said, okay, I'm gonna fix him—by the time they come to New York, I'm gonna know how to chew tobacco myself. And I learned how. When he lined up opposite me that day, he spit, and I spit a hunk of tobacco right back at him. The ball was snapped and we didn't even pay any attention to it. Everybody else was running around out there and we were still in our stances spitting tobacco at each other.

8 More Memories

MEL HEIN: Wartime Commuter

I retired after the 1945 season. But I'd almost gotten out earlier, in 1943. That was after twelve years in the league. I'd taken a job as head football coach up at Union College, in Schenectady, New York. I also taught physical education there—it was a fairly good-paying job because they made me an associate professor. They had to give me that in order to pay the money I wanted. Well, the war was underway, and many students were leaving the campus for military service. We had started with thirty young men on the football team and were down to about eighteen, so I called the president of the university and told him with that few players I didn't feel we could field a football team; others would certainly be going too. He said that I was undoubtedly right and agreed that we should disband the football team for the duration of the war.

Steve Owen saw the announcement in the *New York Times* sports section about Union dropping football, so he called me up and asked me to come back and play again for the Giants.

I said, "No, they're keeping me here to work with the civilian population in physical education, and we're getting some of the military trainees. The government is going to pay half my salary and the university the other half. It's going to be a year-round job."

Steve said, "That's too bad. I was hoping you'd come back because we're losing a lot of our men too." Then he said, "What do you think about just coming down to New York City on Sundays? You could stay in condition up there and just come for the games."

I told him that I did play touch football during the week and I was working out in the phys ed courses that I was running. And, of course, I did miss playing the game. "Let's give it a try," I said.

So I would go down on Friday night after my last class, work out with the team on Saturday, get the new plays, the defenses, and things like that, and then play on Sunday. For three years I played sixty minutes of each game—no preseason games, just the league games for '43, '44, and '45—under those conditions, and then caught the train back to Schenectady after the ball game each Sunday evening. One of the sportswriters dubbed me the "Sunday center."

But it wasn't all that easy. I was getting up in my thirties at the time. In fact, I remember very well my first game. I went into it without any physical contact at all that year. We were up in Boston and our other center, who had worked out with the team in the preseason, was supposed to start until I'd gotten myself into decent shape. But he had gotten hurt in the last preseason game against the Chicago Bears. So I had to start. I played sixty minutes, and I think it was the hottest day Boston ever had. I tell you, it really took a toll on me. I could hardly get on the train to get back to Schenectady that night. It took me about three weeks to get rid of all that soreness and begin to get well. Still, the next week, I had to go the full sixty minutes again. It was a pretty tough time.

CHARLIE CONERLY: Tailback to "T" Quarterback

When they finally switched me from tailback to a T-formation quarterback, it was all new to me. I must say, it wasn't all that easy making the adjustment. You must remember in those days we just came to camp a couple of weeks before the season started, and that's all the time we had to work at making the change. Bobby Layne [with the Detroit Lions] was going through the same thing at the same time, and I know he found it the same way—difficult. It was, in the end, much better for me than the A-formation. And I must admit I was happy with it. It's what enabled me to play so long. That and, of course, the guys who did such a good job blocking for me. That's what kept my career going as long as it did. I believe Sid Luckman and Sammy Baugh said the same thing: switching to the T, where you didn't get hit every play, lengthened their careers too.

I remember once after we were using the T-formation that, for one game, Steve Owen had us go back to the old A-formation. It was against the Chicago Cardinals, and we really confused them. They just didn't know how to defense the A because nobody was using it. We whipped them bad that day [51–21, in 1950].

Sid Luckman, famed Chicago Bears T-formation quarterback drops back to toss one against the Giants in November 1943. It was during this game at the Polo Grounds that Luckman, much to the chagrin of the Giants, set two NFL records—throwing seven touchdown passes and gaining 433 passing yards—in a 56-7 Bears' rout. No. 32 on the Giants is tackle Al Blozis; the Bears' No. 35 is tackle Bill Steinkemper.

ALEX WEBSTER: Running

I was not the fastest of ball carriers. Long yardage was not my plan. Hell, if I could get ten yards on a play I was ecstatic—everything else was a bonus. I think I probably hold the record as a running back for getting caught from behind. The open field was not my country, and if I managed to get into it I thought, Hallelujah!

 I did have a pretty good year in 1955. Eddie Price and Kyle Rote were banged up and didn't carry the ball much. I carried it the most that year [128 times for 634 yards, an average of 5 yards a carry]. After the season I signed a two-year contract.

The next year was a good one too. That was the year we moved to Yankee Stadium, 1956, and it was the year we won the championship. We had played the Bears to a tie in the regular season [17–17]. But we were really up for them in the championship game, and we just walked all over them that day [47–7].

GIANT POET LAUREATE

On the occasion of "Tim Mara Day" at the Polo Grounds in November 1932, Westbrook Pegler, in his syndicated column "Speaking Out," observed a new Giant in the fold:

They have hired cheerleaders from time to time, and yesterday a poet laureate bobbed up in the literature of the official program (price, 15 cents) with a new alma mater song dedicated to Tim Mara, entitled "My Song."

The new alma mater song, struck from the lyre of poet Thomas J. McCarthy, runs about a hundred lines, which is somewhat longer than the formula for such works. . . . A few lines will serve to tell you about the new song:

Each fall my joy is without bounds,

On Sundays at the Polo Grounds.

For when our football Giants play,

Just try to keep this guy away.

It is little better than most college songs but, then, the college poets are amateurs, like the college players, and cannot be expected to write as well as the pros.

DICK MODZELEWSKI: 1958

The best season I can remember in my entire football career was 1958. We had to beat Cleveland three times, which would seem to be impossible—but we did it.

Top it off with the sudden-death championship game against Baltimore. It was such an intense, suspenseful year. Too bad we couldn't have ended it on a better note by winning the championship. We deserved it that year.

They had some tough linemen, the Colts; so did the Browns around that time. You'd never forget going up against Jim Parker of Baltimore or Lou Groza of Cleveland—everybody remembers him as a kicker, but he was a hell of an offensive lineman too.

SAM HUFF: The Colts, 1958

We had a good year in 1958. In fact, I'd say the 1958 and 1959 teams were as good as any football team that ever played in New York. The unfortunate part is those were the greatest teams they ever had in Baltimore, too. Some people feel the Colts of that time were the greatest football team ever to play in the NFL. They had four Hall of Famers on their offensive team alone—Johnny Unitas, Raymond Berry, Lenny Moore, and Jim Parker—and two more on the defensive unit—Gino Marchetti and Art Donovan. And they also had guys like [Alan] Ameche and Big Daddy Lipscomb.

They beat us in '58, but it was in overtime, sudden death. We were winning by three points with about two minutes left; that's when Unitas took them about eighty-five yards and they got a field goal to tie us. There were only seven seconds left when they kicked that field goal. They had the momentum then, and Unitas drove them down the field again in overtime, and they beat us [23–17]. They were a better team than us at the end of that game; that's all there was to it. The difference was Johnny Unitas.

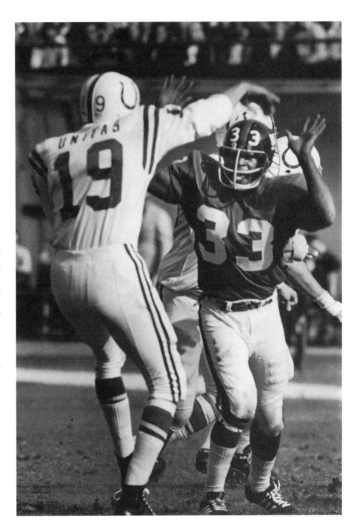

The legendary Johnny Unitas, here in the twilight of his Baltimore Colts career in the early 1970s, still has his inimitable form as he gets one off against the Giants. Applying the pressure is New York safety Joe Green (No. 33).

"He had what a lot of others didn't have— he could fake and bootleg and punt, and he was a great team leader."

–Y. A. TITTLE

We had to play some very good football to get to those two championship games in '58 and '59. We had to beat out the Browns, and they had a very good team, what with Jimmy Brown and Bobby Mitchell and players like that. And, of course, Paul Brown was one of the most highly regarded coaches in the league. But we beat them three times in 1958, one of them a playoff game. We were a better team, though. They built their whole offense around Jim Brown, but we shut him down. [Defensive coach Tom] Landry had analyzed them perfectly; we simply stopped Brown and therefore shut down their offense. They had a great place-kicker, Lou Groza, but so did we—Pat Summerall. Pat kicked that field goal in a snowstorm to win one of those games that year, probably the greatest kick I ever saw. And we beat them both times we played in 1959, the second time by a huge score [48–7].

Y. A. TITTLE on FRANKIE ALBERT

Frankie Albert taught me a lot. He was a master magician as a quarterback in terms of ball handling and leading the football team on the field. He was always very sure of himself. When you start talking about quarterbacks, you have to remember how different it was then from today. Today the plays are sent in from the sideline. We had to be able to throw the ball like they do today, but we had to do a lot of faking, a lot of trickery, and we had to get in the huddle and run the offense; we had to be thinking about what we were going to be doing the down after this as well as this down and make the decisions ourselves. And Albert was probably the best quarterback I saw play in terms of this. I don't mean to say he could play quarterback in the NFL today—he probably couldn't because he didn't throw the ball that well. But in that period he was a true leader. He had what a lot of others didn't have—he could fake and bootleg and punt, and he was a great team leader. I'm disappointed he's not in the Hall of Fame.

MEL HEIN: The Giants in California

Tim Mara was a terrific fellow in many ways. He used to travel with the team but was a New Yorker through and through. In 1934 we won the world championship—we beat the Chicago Bears in the famous "Sneakers Game." In those days, the league champion always went to the West Coast and played two or three postseason exhibition games against an all-star team made up of different players from the National Football League. So we went out there, and we stayed at Pacific

Palisades in a nice hotel overlooking a golf course. It was very beautiful and very quiet, away from the busyness of Los Angeles. Tim had come out with us. Well, after two days in that hotel, he went home. He said he had to get back to New York City. Why? Because it was too quiet in California. He said the birds would wake him up in the morning about six o'clock. Tim said he had to get back to New York, where he was raised on the East Side—and where he could hear the subway and the fire engines and all the racket. He couldn't sleep unless he heard all the noises of New York. So he never did see the game. After two days he was all worn out from the quiet and had to get back so he could get some rest.

RED BADGRO: The Notre Dame All-Stars

I was fortunate to latch onto a very good team. In 1930, we had Benny Friedman at tailback. We also had Steve Owen in the line; he didn't take over full duties as head coach until the following year. We ran second to the Green Bay Packers, as I recall. They had Johnny Blood McNally in his prime and Red Dunn and Cal Hubbard and Lavie Dilweg.

That was also the year we played the special exhibition game at the end of the season against Knute Rockne's all-star team of former Notre Dame players at the Polo Grounds. Tim Mara had arranged it, and the receipts were to go for the benefit of the unemployed in New York City. Rockne had the Four Horsemen there [Harry Stuhldreyer, Elmer Layden, Don Miller, and Jim Crowley] and Hunk Anderson, quite a lineman in his day, and a raft of others. We walloped them pretty good, though [22–0]. There was a huge crowd for it. Mayor [Jimmy] Walker was there and so was Governor Al Smith. And the game earned over $100,000 for the charity.

WELLINGTON MARA: Super Bowl XXV

The first memory that comes to mind is that Desert Storm was going on at the time. We were surrounded by SWAT teams, and airplanes were flying overhead. There was a real worry of a terrorist attack. We had to go through very strict security to even get into the stadium.

Before that, when we were going to San Francisco for the NFC championship game, I remember Parcells telling the players, "Pack for two weeks because we're going direct from there to Tampa" (where Super Bowl XXV was to be played; and there was to be just one week instead of the usual two weeks in between). That was the kind of confidence we had.

The 49ers must have had some confidence, too, because before our game with them they sent their office furniture down to Tampa. When Bill [Parcells] heard about that, he told the team, and added, "They've already written you off!" which, of course, really fired the team up.

On the sideline with an intense Bill Parcells. A native of New Jersey, Parcells was a linebacker at Wichita State, drafted by the Detroit Lions, but instead chose to go into coaching (at Hastings College in Nebraska). He was an assistant coach at Wichita State, Army, Florida State, Vanderbilt, and Texas Tech and head coach at the Air Force Academy before signing on in the NFL. After a year with the New England Patriots, he joined the Giants in 1981 as defensive coordinator and was appointed head coach in 1983.

ALEX WEBSTER: Finishing as a Fullback

In 1961, I was switched to fullback. That was when Jim Lee Howell retired and Lombardi had gone on to Green Bay two years earlier. Allie Sherman was our new

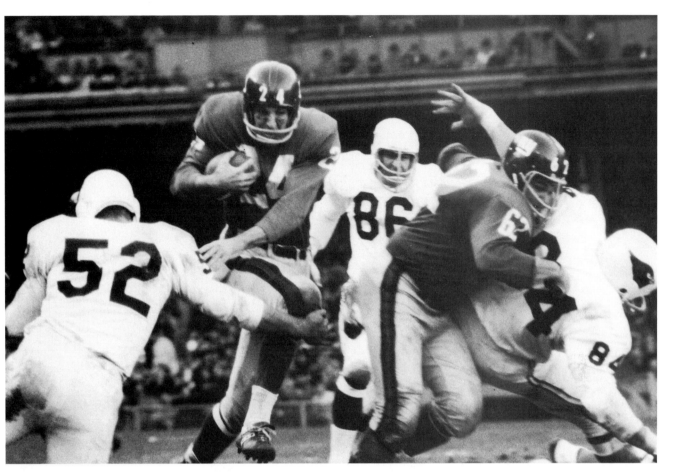

Phil King bursts through the St. Louis line on the heels of a savage block by New York guard Darrell Dess (No. 62). King was the Giants' most productive ground gainer in 1963, rushing for 613 yards and adding another 377 yards on thirty-two pass receptions. New York lost this game, 24–17, the last of only three losses that year. The Cardinals in the picture are Marion Rushing (No. 52) and Joe Robb (No. 84).

head coach. I had been out for most of the 1960 season with a bad knee. We had Phil King and Joe Morrison and Bob Gaiters as halfbacks. Gifford was out that year because of the concussion he got in 1960. So Allie moved me to fullback. I kind of liked it because I was too damn slow to be a receiver and I was weighing around 225 pounds, so fullback seemed like the natural place to switch me to. As it turned out, it was the best year I ever had rushing. I gained 928 yards. At that time the only player with the Giants who had ever gained more in a single season was Eddie Price [971 in 1951].

I had a good year in 1962 as well; that year I gained 743 yards. Y. A. Tittle had been our quarterback in '61 and '62, and one of his favorite plays was to backpedal into the pocket and then toss a little screen pass to me. I was the second-leading receiver on the team in '62 after Del Shofner—I caught forty-seven passes.

Fullback Eddie Price came to the Giants in 1950 from Tulane and averaged 5.6 yards a carry as a rookie, gaining 703 yards rushing (then the third-highest total in club history). The following year he led the NFL with 971 yards. Twice an All-Pro, Price stayed through the 1956 season and ranks seventh in rushing in club annals with 3,292 yards.

In 1963 we won our conference again but got beat by the Bears [14–10] in the championship game. By 1964, I was thirty-three years old and pretty much over the hill; so was most everybody else who was left. Sherman had traded away a lot of ballplayers after the 1963 season, like Sam Huff and Dick Modzelewski. We had a terrible year—we won only two games and for the first time in history ended up in last place. I hung it up as a player after that year.

ARNIE WEINMEISTER: All-Star, 1948

I got to play in the College All-Star Game, which they held every year before the opening of the pro season. It was always played at Soldier Field in Chicago, and they used to draw more than 100,000 for the game. It was quite an event and an honor to be selected to play in it.

The coach of the All-Stars that year [1948] was Frank Leahy of Notre Dame. Well, he picked his own two tackles to start, George Connor and Ziggy Czarobski. But he said to me, "You've impressed me as a football player, young man, and even though you're a tackle I'm going to start you as a guard." So I got to be one of the starting lineup who runs out in the spotlight just before the game—it was always played under the lights at night then.

We had a great team: Johnny Lujack at quarterback, and Charlie Conerly from Ole Miss and Bob Chappius and Bump Elliot from Michigan in the backfield; and also Len Ford from Michigan at end. But we got trimmed and learned what pro football was going to be like. We played the Chicago Cardinals, and they were just too much—they whipped us 28–0.

SHIPWRECK KELLY: 1932

It was Percy Johnson who wanted me to move to New York. He was from Kentucky and like a father to me. He was chairman of the board of the Chemical Bank, a guy like J. P. Morgan—wealthy as hell. When I was in school, he used to come down to Kentucky and watch me play football. He had a son who was my age and in the same class, and we were great friends. I used to go up to New York every summer and stay with them. Then after I graduated, Percy Johnson said, "Come on to New York."

So in the summer of 1932 I came and he gave me a job at the Chemical Bank. I worked there two weeks, I think it was. I saw what it was like and decided I wanted to play pro football. I went to see the people at the Giants, and they offered me a contract, a shitty contract like they all were in those days, but I played. Tim Mara was the man I talked to there, the owner. There was also Jack Mara, his son, and a kid called Wellington Mara, but Tim Mara was the whole thing then.

Steve Owen was the coach, a nice friendly sort of guy; too friendly, in fact, and a lot of the players used to bullshit him a lot because he was too nice sometimes. His brother Bill played on the team and was a pretty good tackle.

I didn't get to play until the second game of the season. It was against Green Bay, and we weren't doing a thing. The Giants hadn't scored a single point in their first game that year, and against Green Bay we hadn't scored one either. So Owen sent me in. I broke a couple of runs, one was about thirty yards, and I caught a couple of passes that day, but we still didn't score a point. But I became a starter after that. I played about six or seven games with the Giants that year, but then I quit because the doctor told me I wasn't in shape for it. I had a small touch of rheumatic fever, and I didn't feel very good—and they weren't paying me very much money anyway. I had some money myself, and so I went back to Kentucky.

FRANK GIFFORD: Coming Back

After I came back in 1962, we had a couple of good years. A lot of people said I should give it up and concentrate on other things. I'd put in nine years and gone to a number of championship games. Some were saying that maybe I would be pressing my luck by going back. But I wasn't totally out of football in 1961—I scouted for the Giants all that year. But I said to myself after I watched the Giants get beat pretty badly in the title game of '61—they lost 37–0—this is kind of ridiculous that I'm not playing. I still had a few more good years in me, I felt. I was in good shape. I'd been working out. And what the hell—I could always do later what I was doing then; the broadcasting business would be there forever. And the overriding thing was, I genuinely missed the game. So I decided to come back.

It was tougher than I thought it would be getting back into shape. You tend to forget how hard the knocks are and how demanding the game of pro football is. But I'm really glad that I did it.

When I came back it wasn't as a halfback, however. It was as a flanker, which suited me fine. I even got invited to the Pro Bowl in '62 as a flanker. It was the third different position I'd gone to the Pro Bowl at: flanker, halfback, and defensive back.

I got to two more championship games as a result of coming back. We played Vince's Packers for the title in 1962, but we lost [16–7]. And we played the Bears

Out of uniform, the Giants' offensive punch of the early 1960s. From left to right: Joe Walton, Joe Morrison, Frank Gifford, and Del Shofner.

the next year for it and lost that, too [14–10]. That year, 1963, was an especially good year for us offensively. We came close to setting an NFL record for points scored in a single season: we scored 448, which was an average of 32 a game [the NFL record at the time was 466, set by the Los Angeles Rams in 1950, an average of 38.8 a game in the then twelve-game regular season; the Houston Oilers had scored 513 points in the AFL in 1961, a 36.6 average per game].

We probably should have beaten the Bears that year. We got off to the lead when Y. A. Tittle threw a touchdown pass to me in the first quarter. But then Y. A. hurt his knee, and he couldn't really get around at all. And our backup quarterback, Glynn Griffing, the only one we had, hadn't even practiced with the team the week before the game because he had gone down to Mississippi to get married; so he wasn't going to be of any help to us. So they just shot up Y. A. and sent him back out there. He tried to hobble through it, but he couldn't really throw the ball. I don't want to take anything away from the Bears. They played a tough game. They had a great defense that year—Bill George, Ed O'Bradovich, Doug Atkins, Richie Petitbon.

After the '63 championship game with the Bears in Chicago, it was pretty much a downhill slide—plummet might be a better word—for the Giants. And I knew it was time to go after the 1964 season.

Off the Field

9

Two Giant youths, Frank Gifford (left) and quarterback Don Heinrich (right), visit with then Vice President Richard Nixon at West Point, where all three were attending President Eisenhower's Youth Fitness Conference.

FRANK GIFFORD's Visitor

While Frank Gifford was having his injured knee attended to in a New York hospital in 1958, he awoke at about five-thirty one morning to find a large, trembling young man at the foot of his bed. The immobilized Gifford watched as the man shook the bed and ranted, "What's the matter with your Giants? What's the matter with all of you, Gifford?"

The man walked over to the venetian blinds and ran his hand up and down them to make noise. "What you need is someone like me, a killer. I was in Korea."

Gifford grabbed the water pitcher beside his bed. "If he was going to come at me, I was going to gong him," Gifford said later. The man didn't, but he also did not leave. He just stood there, running his hands along the blinds.

Gifford finally said, "If you really think you can help the team, get your ass down to Yankee Stadium. Tell them what you can do." The man sort of nodded and left, much to Gifford's relief.

However, the man did take the Giff's advice and went to Yankee Stadium. He managed to get into the locker room, where most of the players by that time were suiting up for practice, and began screaming, first at 260-pound Dick Modzelewski and then at some others. According to New York sportswriter Barry Gottherer, the man then began drop-kicking footballs around the room, castigating the team before several policemen arrived to take him away.

As the man was leaving, Gottherer quoted him as shouting back, "All right, so you don't appreciate me. I'll go down to Baltimore and help Johnny Unitas out."

DICK MODZELEWSKI: Night before the Big Game

I was probably the biggest jokester on the team—along with Sam Huff anyway. I remember in 1956 before the championship game my brother Ed drove my car in from Pittsburgh and stayed a night or two with us. We were not staying in the hotel at that time; we were on our own until Sunday morning. There was a bunch of us—Sam Huff, Bill Svoboda, Ed, and some others—who stayed up playing poker. And Ed kept saying, "Aren't you guys going to bed? You're playing for the championship tomorrow!"

He was in the locker room before the game the next day and most of us were clowning around. He just kept shaking his head. Ed was with Cleveland then, and he kept saying Paul Brown would never let this go on. Finally he said to me, "You guys are gonna get the shit beat out of you today. You're nowhere serious enough." Instead, we went out and beat the crap out of the Bears [47–7].

SHIPWRECK KELLY in New York

New York was a great place to be back then. I had a helluva life. I really was a protégé of Percy Johnson—and if you're a protégé of someone like that you can tell everybody to kiss your ass. I met all kinds of people through him—the socialites, the big people on Wall Street. I nearly married Bill Woodworth's daughter around then. Bill Woodworth was one of the biggest bankers in the world then—had houses in three or four places.

I was having a great time. [Dan] Topping [who would later own the New York Yankees baseball team] and I were all over Broadway. He loved the showgirls.

We used to go to the nightclubs around New York all the time too, but not during the times I was playing football—at least not a lot. I was serious about football. The one that was my favorite was the Stork Club because Sherman

Billingsley liked me. He owned it and he had piles of money. I used to go in there and if I wanted any money he'd give it to me and say, "Pay me back when you're ready." He did the same thing for Walter Winchell and a lot of other people who went in there.

The hot-shit place of them all, though, was El Morocco. I knew John Perona, the owner there, and he was very nice to me. The big thing was to get into the nightclub; and even then only if you were a hot shit would you be sitting where the hot shits were. If you were not, they'd put you in the back or in a corner somewhere out of the way.

I remember one night in the El Morocco when I was with four or five people at one table. In walked this guy with a beard—there weren't many beards in those days—and John Perona came over and said to me, "Do you know who that guy is?"

I said I didn't.

"It's Orson Welles, the actor."

On second thought, I said, I thought I'd seen a picture of him somewhere. So Perona brought Orson Welles over to the table and introduced him to us. I tried to be a smart aleck, like I did a lot of times in those days. I said, "Gee, Mr. Welles, it's nice meeting someone like you." He didn't know who I was or that I played football or anything about me. But he was very pleasant. Then I said something like, "Why do you cultivate something on your face that grows wild on your ass?"

"Mr. Kelly," he said, "you are new in New York, and if I were you I wouldn't tell my friends how much you know about my ass."

I felt like shit and got up and left.

I didn't let that crap interfere with my football playing, however; I kept the two apart. You had to because it was a rugged game, much tougher than college ball. The sons of bitches in the pros were bigger and stronger and all of them were pretty damn good, whereas in college only two or three players on a team might be worth a shit.

Off the Field with **ANDY ROBUSTELLI**

We were very parochial in those days, our social lives pretty simple. Being out late was not something you did a lot, and very rarely was anybody fined. Modzelewski would sit around and sing in Polish, Grier would play his guitar all night until you might want to kill him, and we'd go out for a couple of beers, but that was about the extent of the excitement. Some of us used to go to Toots Shor's, however. That was the one place that most of us liked to go. Toots always liked the athletes and

On the sideline—waiting. Three of the famous front four: Jim Katcavage (No. 75), Andy Robustelli (No. 81), and Dick Modzelewski (No. 77).

looked after us—getting us a table, things like that. He made you feel like you were a little special.

HARRY NEWMAN's New York

I roomed with Kink Richards when I first joined the Giants. He was a helluva blocking back for us. Ken Strong came to the Giants that year too; he'd been playing with the Staten Island Stapes before that. Ken, of course, was a magnificent football player and a fine guy. I used to pal around with him quite a bit. Some others who were good friends then were Mel Hein and Ray Flaherty and Red Badgro. Mel was a true All-Pro at center, and Flaherty and Badgro were two of the best ends in the league.

When training camp was over, I lived in New York at a place called the Broadway View Hotel. Then I moved to the Terrace Hotel, which was over on Ninety-sixth and Riverside Drive. We didn't do too much carousing in those days. Some maybe, but during the season we were all pretty dedicated. We wanted to win, and we knew we were a good enough team to win.

N. Y. GIANTS
·vs·
DETROIT LIONS

Price 10 cents

POLO GROUNDS

Sunday, November 1, 1936

KINK RICHARDS
Star Giant Back

Sunday, November 8, 1936, Kickoff 2:15 P. M.
AT POLO GROUNDS
NEW YORK GIANTS vs. CHICAGO BEARS

His name was Elvin Richards, but he was better known around the Polo Grounds as "Kink." He worked his way out of obscurity (Simpson College in Iowa) in 1933 and into a backfield with such luminaries as Ken Strong, Harry Newman, and Dale Burnett. Richards became the second Giant to rush for more than one hundred yards in a game, a feat he accomplished against the Brooklyn Dodgers in 1933 only a week after Harry Newman became the first to reach the century standard. Richards led the club in rushing in 1935, with 449 yards, and stayed around through the 1939 season.

And we did win that year, at least we won the Eastern Division. We only lost three of fourteen games. In one game we set a record when we beat the Philadelphia Eagles 56–0. We split with the Chicago Bears during the regular season—they beat us at Wrigley Field in Chicago [14–10], and we won at the Polo Grounds [3–0]. They won the NFL West, and we played them in what was the first official championship game in the NFL—it was the first year the league was broken into two separate divisions. They had Bronko Nagurski and Red Grange and Jack Manders—a really fine team.

PAT SUMMERALL's Foot

I got into what you might call semi-organized football in junior high school down in Lake City in northern Florida—the town where I was born and raised. In high school, of course, it was well organized. Down there, it was one of the things you just did if you were one of the bigger guys in the class—you sort of had an obligation to play.

It was in high school that I really got to love playing football. I had had a rather unfortunate childhood. I was born with a clubfoot—the right one. Basically it was turned around backwards. At that time, the way they treated it was by breaking both bones in the bottom of the leg and just turning the foot around. The doctor told my mother afterwards that I would be able to walk but I would probably never be able to run or play with other kids. As time passed, however, through nature's help and the good Lord's help, it got better and better. And as it turned out, that was the foot I used to kick with—although that was way down the road.

By the time I got to high school, things had pretty well worked out. I was on the track team and ran the 100-yard dash and the 440. I ran the 100 in about 10.1, which at that time was considered pretty good. I also played baseball and, of course, football. And actually, my best sport in high school was basketball.

MEL HEIN in the '30s

The closeness of the Giants team in the 1930s was one of the reasons we did so well. There was a lot of team spirit and togetherness. Most of the players lived in the same area—between 100th and 103rd streets around Broadway. We stayed in about three different hotels up there. I stayed the longest at the old Whitehall Hotel at 100th and Broadway, and a number of others did, too. It was a small hotel, and each room had its own kitchenette. Steve Owen lived there all year round with his wife; he had the penthouse. He liked to have his players nearby and usually tried to talk them all into staying at the Whitehall. After the season, of course, all the ballplayers went back to their hometowns. There were a few players who didn't want to live in a hotel, and they got apartments of their own; but still they were within two or three blocks of us. That worked out quite well in bringing us all kind of close, and we got to know each other personally and to know each other's families. It unified us in a way that a lot of other teams were not able to accomplish. That and the winning attitude that Steve gave to us was what made us a winning football team.

LOONEY as in JOE DON

Frank Gifford, in his book *Gifford on Courage*, wrote of what it was like dealing with Joe Don Looney, the unorthodox (to put it mildly) running back out of Oklahoma who was the first-round draft choice of the Giants in 1964.

He had the potential to be an extraordinary player. But—there were problems. He injured his leg early in training camp. So [coach Allie] Sherman told him to see the trainer about it. To Allie's amazement, Looney refused.

His reason? "It's my leg. I know more about it than the trainer."

He wouldn't go to Detroit for an exhibition game. "I can't play; why should I go?" he asked me.

The brain trust of the Giants circa the late 1930s. From right to left: Wellington Mara (secretary), Tim Mara (founder), Jack Mara (president), Steve Owen (coach).

"You're part of the team," I said.

"I'm not part of the team if I can't play," he replied.

Joe Don came in an hour after curfew one night and was fined. "Not fair," he said. "I was in bed an hour early last night, so we should be even up."

He wouldn't throw his used socks into a marked bin because "I'm not going to do what any sign tells me to do."

Although I didn't see it, I understand that in scrimmages he often ran one way when the play called for him to go another. His reason: "Anybody can run where the blockers are. A good football player makes his own holes."

As a last-ditch measure, Wellington Mara and Allie Sherman asked Y. A. [Tittle] and me to try to talk to the young man. Joe Don was 6'1", 224 pounds and ran the hundred in something like 9.7. They wanted to keep him.

We were still in training camp at Fairfield [Connecticut] University. Joe Don was lying down in his room listening to music when we found him.

Y. A. flopped on the other bed and started to tell Joe Don about his trade to New York from San Francisco, which somehow Y. A. equated with Looney's problems: how difficult it was leaving the team where he had spent most of his career, his family, his business; being traded for a rookie lineman; coming to a team in a strange city with a popular quarterback [Charlie Conerly] ahead of him; and how "alone" Y. A. had felt.

Clearly talking from his heart and, perhaps for the first time outside of his family, discussing his gut feeling about the trade, Tittle went on for about twenty minutes with Joe Don and me listening intently.

Finally, Y. A. finished and stopped—serious, sad, thinking of what had happened just three years earlier.

Joe Don broke an embarrassing silence. He sat up, completely caught up in Tittle's reverie, and said sympathetically, "It must have been really tough, Y. A. Anything I can do for you?"

The counsel of Tittle and Gifford evidently failed, because Joe Don Looney was traded to the Baltimore Colts before the opening game of the 1964 regular season.

HARRY NEWMAN: Hold-Out, 1935

In 1935, I had a contract dispute with the Maras. I decided to hold out. In that last game that I played in, in 1934, the one against the Bears, we filled the Polo Grounds. Because I was on a percentage, they had to pay me a lot of dough. As a result, they wouldn't give me the same kind of contract for the next year.

Also that year before, they had a fund-raising game for Mayor Cavanaugh—I think that was his name. He was a famous World War I hero, and it was a benefit for him and charity. They had a sellout for it, and I donated my entire salary for that game to the benefit. They [the Maras] never said anything about that when contract negotiations came around.

I held out, but it didn't do me a lot of good. The season started, and I kept myself sort of busy scouting for Coach [Harry] Kipke of Michigan. I scouted teams like Columbia. But finally I had to do something, so I came back and played out the year with the Giants. I alternated with Danowski that year, but I felt my days with the Giants were over. They were never going to pay me the money I wanted. I knew that.

> "They were never going to pay me the money I wanted. I knew that."
>
> —HARRY NEWMAN

A grand reunion. At Giants Stadium, the stars of the 1960s come back and take a plainclothes bow: from left, Ben Agajanian, Andy Robustelli, Rosey Grier, Herb Rich, Jim Katcavage, Kyle Rote, Charlie Conerly, Jack Stroud.

JIM KATCAVAGE: Commuting

From the beginning, I used to commute to New York from Philadelphia. I'd take the train over to Penn Station and then the subway up to Yankee Stadium. I did that for eighteen years—thirteen as a player and five as a coach. Emlen Tunnell was from Philly too, and we used to ride over together until he retired, which was after the 1958 season. We were the best of friends. Emlen was truly a great ballplayer. He was a walk-on back in 1948. He had played at Iowa, but around that time there were very few blacks in the NFL. He asked for a tryout, made the team, and went on to the Hall of Fame. I played with him his last three years in New York. When Lombardi left in 1959, he took Emlen along with him to Green Bay. Tunnell was just an extraordinary athlete—a super defensive back, and no one could return punts and kickoffs like him. On top of that, he was just one hell of a nice guy who everybody on the team really liked to have around.

RED BADGRO: On Dr. March

In that time of the Depression, a player needed to work in the off-season too, and I did as much as I could; but it was hard to pick up a job. Times were tough for everybody.

Dr. Harry March, a grand old fellow, was running the Giants for Tim Mara when I came to them in 1930. One thing I'll never forget about him: I got my chin cut open in practice one day, and I needed eleven stitches to close it up. I just went by his office, and he didn't have any of his medical equipment with him, so he got a plain needle and sewing thread out of his drawer and sewed up my chin. He liked football more than the practice of medicine, I believe.

PAT SUMMERALL: Touch Football

One game I got a great kick out of was not an NFL one. We played a touch football game in Central Park in New York, a kind of gimmick to celebrate the twentieth anniversary of the championship game of 1958. It started out lighthearted and then we all got kind of serious, pretty competitive. Johnny Unitas threw a couple of touchdown passes. They won, and I remember saying as we walked off the field, "I'll be damned—we couldn't cover Raymond Berry twenty years ago, and we still can't."

MEL HEIN: Money and Decisions

I stayed with the Giants all those years because I wanted to. I was satisfied with New York. The Maras treated me very well; but as far as salaries went, well, we went back and forth a few times. One year in particular, 1938, after we had won the NFL title, I asked for a certain amount of money, like three hundred dollars a ball game. I asked Jack Mara for it, and I got a telegram back from him: he offered me a contract, but the amount was not exactly what I'd asked for.

I said no. Then he offered me a season contract, flat sum for the year, but it also turned out to be less than what I'd wanted. So finally I got teed off and started looking around for something else. Well, the Los Angeles Bulldogs, out on the West Coast, was a pro team but not an NFL team, and the owner offered to get me a year-round job at a tire and rubber company out there if I played for the Bulldogs. Financially it looked pretty good. Well, after about five different telegrams from Jack Mara with offers, all of which I turned down, I finally sent a telegram to him that said, "Don't send any more telegrams or call me. My mind is definitely made up. I'm going to stay out on the Pacific Coast."

Right away, boom—I got another telegram from Jack with the salary I wanted.

Another time, I decided I wanted to get into coaching, perhaps on the college level. So I talked to Lou Little, who was head coach then at Columbia, which wasn't far from where we were staying in New York—up around 150th Street. Lou had been president of the coaches' association that year, and they were having their national meeting out in Los Angeles. I asked him if I could come out there and hang around the hotel and maybe meet some of the head coaches. He said, "Sure, Mel—come on out and hang around, and I'll find out if there are any positions that are open. I'm sure we can help you."

This all took place right near the end of our season. Well, the Giants had a breakfast at our hotel after the last game of the season, before all the players started heading back for their homes. Tim Mara, who knew I was thinking about going from a player to a coach, said to me, "Mel, I want you to sign a three-year contract with us for five thousand dollars a season."

That was real big money in those days. I couldn't believe it. I said, "Sure, glad to!"

I lived on the seventh floor of that hotel, and I ran up the stairs, didn't even wait for the elevator, and showed my wife a check for five hundred dollars and told her about the five thousand dollar contract. Then I called Lou Little and told him I wouldn't be seeing him out in Los Angeles. That's how you got your raises in those days; it was a little different from the way they do business these days.

10
After the Game Is Over

"I had always
thought when
I finally hung it
up that I would
go back home
to Florida
and tend to
some business
interests."

—PAT SUMMERALL

Y. A. TITTLE: Time to Retire, 1964

In 1964 I got hurt probably the worst of all my seventeen years in pro football. I got hit by John Baker of the Steelers in the second game of the season and it crushed all my rib cartilage. It was really hard to breathe after that, and every time I got knocked down it was really hard to get up. I played, but I was a sitting duck again. You couldn't get novocaine in there, so I was really limited in what I could do; as a result I had a very poor year.

After that, I knew it was time to quit—especially when I saw our other quarterback, Gary Wood, was wanting to date my daughter.

After football, I opened my insurance business in California, and I helped coach the San Francisco 49ers.

PAT SUMMERALL Auditions

As my career in football was winding down, I began another in broadcasting. The way it came about was that we had played the Green Bay Packers in a preseason exhibition game in Newark and were training at that time in Bear Mountain, New York, near West Point. The game was on a Friday night, and we did not have to be back at camp for practice until Monday night. So a bunch of us got together and went into Manhattan for the weekend. I was rooming with Charlie Conerly. I was lying on a bed watching television, and he was in the shower. The phone rang and I answered it, and this gentleman, who I didn't know, asked for Charlie. I said he was in the shower, and he asked, "Well, who is this?" I told him and he said to remind Charlie that he was supposed to come to CBS that afternoon at four o'clock to read for this radio show.

I was maybe an inch away from hanging up the phone when he said, "Hey, wait a minute. What are you doing this afternoon?"

My answer was, "I don't know. I'm either going to a movie or get together with the guys and go drink beer somewhere."

He said, "Well, why don't you come along and take the audition too?"

I said, "Why not?" As it turned out, there were four of us who went over there. And I ended up getting the job.

By the time I retired after the 1961 season, I'd been with CBS for several years. I guess I had always thought when I finally hung it up that I would go back home to Florida and tend to some business interests and maybe teach school. But when it became a reality, I said to my wife, "Look, I like this broadcasting business. It's

Life on the football field was a total and brutal commitment for thirty-seven-year-old Y. A. Tittle, a fierce and unyielding competitor. No words can portray his commitment more dramatically than this now-classic photo of a bloodied, frustrated, exhausted Tittle in the end zone after suffering an especially savage hit in a 1964 game at Pittsburgh. (Photo Courtesy of the *Pittsburgh Post-Gazette*)

something I think I can do. But to do it, we're going to have to move up to New York full time." Which we did.

TOM LANDRY: Leaving the Field for the Sideline

I stopped playing after the 1955 season. The next year I just coached, and that was the year we beat the Bears for the NFL championship [47–7]. And I will say both our defense and offense were superb that day. I stayed on as defensive coordinator for three more years.

In the off season, I was living in Dallas. I'd moved there in 1955. I was very familiar with the people who were starting up the Dallas Cowboys—Clint Murchison, the owner, and Tex Schramm, who was going to run it for him. I believe it was Clint and some others behind the team down there in Dallas who got Tex to come to me about taking the head coach job there in their first season, 1960. I don't know whether Tex might have gone that way—after all, I was just an assistant coach, and I think maybe he might have wanted an experienced head coach to get the new team off the ground.

At the time, too, I was actually thinking about getting out of football altogether. During the off season a while back I'd gotten a degree in industrial engineering in addition to my degree from the University of Texas, and so I was thinking about a life other than football. But then Tex came out and we talked, and he offered me the job. I said to my wife, "Oh, well, we might just as well try it. We'll probably be fired in two or three years, but what the heck." So I agreed and we signed a contract. And my days with the Giants came to an end.

HARRY NEWMAN: Another AFL

Along with a couple of others, I started the American Football League [an earlier AFL, launched in 1936]. Ken Strong came along into the new league, and so did Red Badgro. We had teams in six cities: New York, Brooklyn, Rochester, Cleveland, Pittsburgh, and Boston. I started the team in Brooklyn and we called ourselves the Tigers. The second year of the league, 1937, my franchise moved up to Rochester. We didn't have many big-name players—most were right out of college, and they were the ones who didn't make the NFL. We didn't draw very well either in Brooklyn [perhaps because they were 0–6–1] or Rochester. [After that season the Rochester franchise folded.] Those were still the Depression years, and we just couldn't make a dent in the NFL—which, incidentally, wasn't doing all that well either.

After the Rochester team went under, I left football. I went back to Detroit, my hometown, and went to work for the Ford Motor Company. I was in the sales department at first, but soon I worked into a position where I represented the company over at the state capital in Lansing. I was basically a lobbyist for Ford at that time.

In 1946 I opened my own Ford dealership in Detroit. A few years later I opened another one in Denver, Colorado.

Coach **MODZELEWSKI**

I played three years with the Browns and then retired after the 1966 season. It was time. I'd been in the league since 1953. As Charlie Conerly said, "When you're sore the day of the game, it's time to quit." I was sore the day of every game in 1966.

The restaurant Ed and I owned—Mo and Junior's was the name of it—was a success. We had it for sixteen years. When the Giants would come to town to play Cleveland, they would all come to it for dinner. We'd have people lined up in the streets to see the guys like Gifford and Robustelli and Summerall. Then in the summer when the Yankees would come to play the Indians, we used to get a lot of their ballplayers coming in: Yogi Berra, Mickey Mantle, Moose Skowron.

After I quit playing, I did some scouting for the Browns. In 1968, I got calls from the 49ers, the Steelers, and Art Modell of the Browns about coaching their defensive lines. I signed with the Browns and coached there for ten years. After that I was an assistant coach with the Detroit Lions and Cincinnati Bengals. I coached a total of twenty-two years, and the last eight of them I was the defensive coordinator.

I've been associated with a lot of different teams in the NFL, playing and coaching. But even though I got traded and was mad as hell about it, I still look upon myself as a New York Giant. And I'm proud to be able to say it.

CHARLIE CONERLY: Changing of the Guard

After each season I'd go back to Clarksdale [Mississippi]. There weren't any kind of decent jobs you could get for half the year, so I just played golf every day. I also had bought a little farm from the bonus money I got when I first signed, and my dad farmed it.

After the 1960 season and the problems I was having with my elbow, when they asked me if I was going to come back, I said, "Well, I don't know. I think maybe I've had enough." I'd been with them through thirteen years by then. But we talked, and I finally said I would come back for 1961 but then that would be it.

So in '61 they traded to bring Y. A. Tittle to the Giants. Y. A. and I had played against each other in college—he was at Louisiana State when I was with Ole Miss. Then we'd been playing against each other after he went with the 49ers.

I'm glad they did bring Y. A. in because he was a mighty fine quarterback. I started the first game that year; but in the second, I threw a pass out in the flat and it was intercepted. Allie Sherman, who was our head coach then, pulled me out. Y. A. came on and threw a bunch of passes to Del Shofner and brought the team back so Pat Summerall could kick a field goal for us to win the game.

It was the right thing to do. I was about thirty-eight years old by that time, and Y. A. was just a fine quarterback with a few more good years ahead of him. And he certainly was a big help to the Giants for the next three years. I still to this day cannot understand why San Francisco let him go. But I'm sure glad they did, and so were the Giants.

After I left the Giants I didn't do anything much for the next year. Then I went into the shoe business down in Mississippi, which turned out to be just fine for me, and I stayed with that until I retired in 1984.

Now I'm just taking it easy down here in the same town where I was born—Clarksdale. My wife and I do some traveling, and I get together with some of the old ballplayers in different places, and I get back to New York for some of the Giants' games and some of their alumni functions. I like to see them all. We can still kick around the stories about the way it was.

I played golf the other day with Wellington Mara over in Florida. That was really nice. And I'll be damned—I didn't know he could play that well.

SHIPWRECK KELLY: The Spy

After I got out of football I married Brenda Frazier. And after that I did some work for the FBI [just before and during World War II]. I traveled everywhere for them. You see, I could because of the society that I hung around in. I mean, I went to Europe, to Cuba, then to Mexico, to Peru, to Chile, and when we got in the war I spent a lot of time in Argentina. I could meet people at parties and things—the big shots there—because of my connections. An ordinary person didn't have access to them. But I did. There were loads of rich Germans in Argentina and high-ranking officers, all in that same international society. I would try to find out about the ships, the submarines—things like that—that were off our coasts. And there were a lot of them. A lot of those people knew where they were. I kissed everybody's ass in Argentina to find out things like that, and I found out a lot. I also found out who else was sympathetic to the Germans in that society. I worked at it all the way through the war for Hoover. Then I got out of that part of it. He [J. Edgar Hoover] and I were good friends, did things together many times in the years after the war.

But football was great. It helped me in a lot of ways. I tried to do my job right in the years I played. And it's nice to be remembered for that part of my life.

FRANK GIFFORD: The Broadcaster

After football, it was the broadcast business. I'd been with WCBS while I was playing. I'd started there doing local news for them back in 1962 while there was a

Frank Gifford, shown here in the last year of his playing career, gathers in a pass in a 1964 game against the Cowboys. From the Polo Grounds and Yankee Stadium to the Pro Football Hall of Fame and the Monday Night Football broadcast booth, Gifford has truly left his imprint on the game of professional football.

newspaper strike in New York. After that, they decided to expand their news reporting to include sports and weather. And after I finished playing I began broadcasting NFL games.

I stayed with that until Roone Arledge asked me to be part of the NFL *Monday Night Football* team. Actually, he asked me in 1970, the year it began, but I couldn't take it because of my other contractual obligations. But the following year I was able to. Keith Jackson did it with Howard [Cosell] and Don [Meredith] the first year. Keith's nose was kind of out of joint when I came over the next year, but it all worked out very well. He went over to broadcasting college football, which he does very well.

ARNIE WEINMEISTER: Bad Parting

I left the Giants after the 1953 season. In fact, I had informed them before the season that this was going to be my last season with them.

We had had a terrible year—won only three out of twelve games, which only served to confirm my decision to leave New York. In addition, I had heard about the start-up of a team in Vancouver in the Canadian Football League. I talked to them, and they offered me a position as player-coach at quite a bit more money than I was being paid by the Giants.

The Giants had told me they were not going to give me an increase for the 1954 season even if I decided to come back for another year. So I reiterated to them at the end of the 1953 season that that was my last with them.

The Giants took me to court for supposedly breaking my contract under the option clause where they have a perpetual ownership of you. However, a conversation I had had with the owners of the club [Jack and Wellington Mara] before the 1953 season was confirmed by a letter in which I asked earlier what my status with the club was, because at that time I had been offered an assistant coaching job at the University of Washington. I wanted to know if I would be able to accept it or not. They responded with a letter that contained substantive proof that I had informed them 1953 was to be my last season with the Giants—and that I was free to take the other job. When they came to court in Seattle, they lost the case. And I went up to Canada for two more years of football.

After football, I joined the Teamsters union as an organizer in the San Francisco Bay area. I worked my way up to director of the thirteen western states and was second vice president on the executive board. I stayed with the Teamsters for thirty-six years and retired in March 1992.

ROSEY BROWN: Coach/Scout

After the 1965 season I had to retire from playing. I developed a case of phlebitis, which is an inflammation of a vein, and that prevented me from playing. I was only thirty-two at the time, 1966, and thought if it weren't for the phlebitis, maybe I could get in a few more years. But it wasn't to be.

I stayed with the Giants, though, as an assistant coach until 1971, coaching under Allie Sherman and Alex Webster. That year, 1971, I started as a full-time scout for the team. As a scout, I worked for Jim Lee Howell, who had coached me for a good part of my career [1954–60].

DICK LYNCH: Deciding to Retire

I decided to retire after the 1966 season. I'd been around for nine years, and '66 had been less than memorable. We only won one game, lost twelve, and tied one. And I was pretty established in business by that time.

Still, it's hard to walk away from the game. I remember Harland Svare, who was one of our linebackers when I first came to the Giants, asked me to come back and play and coach for another year. He'd just taken over as the Giants' defensive coach. At the time I was working for Shorewood Press in the printing business, and I was making more money there than I was playing football.

I thought about it. I still was tempted. I got up one morning and put on the workout suit. I was halfway out the door when my wife said something like, "What the hell are you doing?" I said I was going out, get a little in shape; maybe I could do one or two more years—might be fun, might be . . . Well, she gave me about five quick reasons why it wasn't a good idea, the last being my neck—the paralysis thing. "But it's your decision, dear," or something like that, is what she left me with.

Well, I started jogging, and they all fell into place—each concern, or suggestion, whatever it was she laid out. Plus, after about three blocks of running I could really feel it—feel what it would be like if I tried to come back for another year.

"And your neck, dear," she'd said as I went out that day. I thought about that and knew it was over. I turned around and went home, and that was it.

ALEX WEBSTER: The Business World

I left the Giants as head coach after the 1973 season. The next year I did the wrap-up of the Giants' games on television. After that I got into the printing busi-

Two Giant greats of the late 1950s and early '60s, fullback Alex Webster (No. 29) and middle linebacker Sam Huff (No. 70), watch from the sideline of Yankee Stadium.

ness, mostly in the sales end. I went to work for a printing company that was run by Ralph Guglielmi, who had been a great quarterback at Notre Dame and came up with the Redskins the same year I joined the Giants, 1955. He later played with the Giants [1962–63] and a bunch of other NFL teams.

After that I went to work with a food company, Standard Brands, in public relations; they were bought out by Nabisco, and then the whole thing was bought out by R. J. Reynolds, the tobacco company. We had a lot of sports people affiliated with the company—Frank Gifford, Jack Nicklaus, me.

After that I went down to Florida, to a town called Tequesta, near Jupiter, just north of Palm Beach, and opened a restaurant there called Alex Webster's.

There are a lot of us down here in Florida—Pat Summerall, Joe Namath, Bill Parcells, Phil Simms—almost NFL south. We're all still very much in touch with the NFL.

RED BADGRO: Life after the Giants

I found out that the Brooklyn Dodgers, Dan Topping's team [bought a few years earlier from pal and former Giant Shipwreck Kelly], had picked up my option, and so I went over there and played one more year in the NFL.

After Brooklyn, I went back to Southern Cal to get the couple of units I still needed to graduate. After that I went to Ventura Junior College in California and coached football, baseball, and basketball. While I was there, I was contacted by Lou Little, the great coach at Columbia. He used to come over from Columbia to watch the pro games when I was with the Giants. He wanted to know if I would like to come back east to Columbia and be his assistant football coach. I went back there and stayed in that capacity for five years.

After that, it was back across the country to the West Coast, where I coached football at the University of Washington as an assistant for eight years. Then I went to work for the Department of Agriculture in the state of Washington until I retired.

Between playing and coaching, I guess I spent about twenty-five years in football. I hold a lot of fine memories from it.

JIM KATCAVAGE: Leaving

After the 1968 season, I thought I had one more in me. I was thirty-four, but I still felt pretty good. We ended up with a new coach that year—1969. After we lost all our preseason games, Allie Sherman was canned and Alex Webster, who was an assistant then, was moved up to head coach. Right after the appointment, Alex came up to me and asked if I would be his defensive line coach. It was kind of like the handwriting on the wall: "We don't think you'll be playing much anymore. We want you to coach, but we don't want you to play."

The Giants had drafted Fred Dryer that year. He was a highly regarded defensive end out of San Diego State who was their first-round draft pick. It was clear Alex wanted him to start. Dryer was a big guy, tall, about 6'6", and he was good. He went on to become much better known after football when he starred in *Hunter* on television. So I got to coach "Hunter" the three years he was with the Giants. I don't think I had any effect on his acting abilities, though.

I coached in New York through the 1973 season; after Webster resigned I moved to Philadelphia, where I became a scout for the Eagles for the next thirteen years. After that, Art McNally, the NFL's head coach of officials, hired me to scout

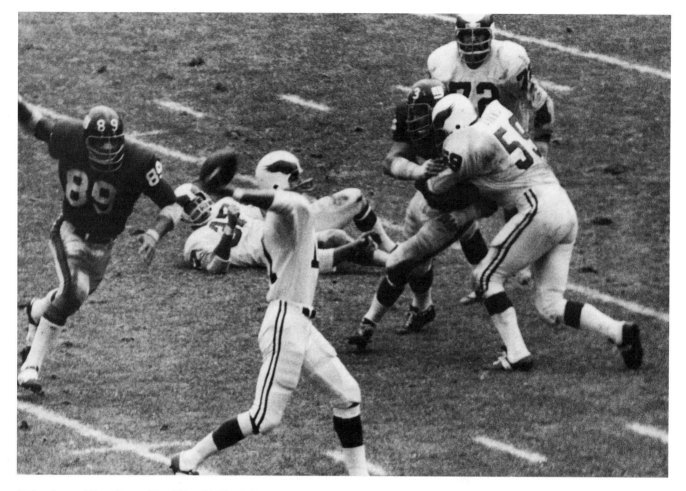

Defensive end Fred Dryer (No. 89), with his sights set on St. Louis Cardinal quarterback Jim Hart here, was the Giants first round draft pick in 1969. He played for the Giants through the 1972 season before being traded to the Los Angeles Rams and subsequently developing a career as an actor in television and the movies.

officials for the league, take a look at those guys officiating in college games, and do some other things related to officiating—something I'm still doing for the league today.

ANDY ROBUSTELLI: The Entrepreneur

I didn't have any trouble with the decision to retire. In 1964 we had a bum season [2–10–2] and I was thirty-eight years old and it was my fourteenth year in the NFL. I knew it was time. My biggest decision was whether to stay in football in some other capacity. My business in the off season [sports marketing] was doing well. I'd started it my first year out in Los Angeles, 1951. It began as a sports store. I started it with the championship-game check I got that year when we beat the Browns. It was small and I didn't take a salary. But it got bigger, branched out, once I moved to New York. It kept me busy during the off season.

I decided to devote my time to the business rather than stay in football. I did, however, come back to serve in the Giants' front office in the 1970s as director of operations.

In the Booth with **KYLE ROTE**

After I retired from playing, I coached the backfield for the Giants in 1962 and 1963. I liked that a lot. There were some moments when you would be watching the backs and flankers and you would wish that you could still be doing the kinds of things they could. But overall at that point I did not miss playing.

I had been doing some radio work while I was still playing, an after-game show for WNEW in New York, the station that broadcast our games. And that enabled me to segue from football into broadcasting full time. I would do the nightly news on radio and the color for the Giants' games. I continued to do that for a number of years after I retired from the Giants. In 1967, I went to NBC.

Later, my wife and I formed our own business, Ronina Chemical Company—we specialize in the processes of breaking precious metals out of ores. That business occupies most of my time these days.

But, I must say, football with the Giants was a great eleven-year ride, and I'm certainly glad I had the opportunity to be along for it.

> "You would be watching the backs and flankers and you would wish that you could still be doing the kinds of things they could."
>
> —KYLE ROTE